Divorce

Divorce

How to help yourself and your finances

Sarah Pennells

A & C Black • London

First published in Great Britain 2008

A & C Black Publishers Ltd
38 Soho Square, London W1D 3HB
www.acblack.com

A CIP record for this book is available from the British Library.

ISBN: 9-781-4081-0113-1

This book is produced using paper that is made from wood grown in
managed, sustainable forests. It is natural, renewable and recyclable.
The logging and manufacturing processes conform to the
environmental regulations of the country of origin.

Design by Fiona Pike, Pike Design, Winchester
Typeset by RefineCatch Limited, Bungay, Suffolk
Printed in the United Kingdom by CPI Bookmarque, Croydon

Contents

Acknowledgements

In writing this book, I have been generously helped by many experts in this field, but the person who deserves special thanks is David Allison, who is a partner with the specialist law firm Family Law in Partnership and a trained mediator. David always made time to offer his expertise – despite his own busy work schedule – both with the legal detail of divorce and by giving me an insight into the realities of advising someone whose marriage is ending on how to deal with the legal and financial consequences.

I am grateful to many others who gave me the benefits of their knowledge and experience, including James Pirrie of Family Law in Partnership; Rachael Kelsey, a partner at Edinburgh law firm Pagan Osborne; Judith Brown, at Belfast law firm Alan M Brown; Karen Ritchie of independent financial advisers Financial Planning for Women; Gareth Woodward, a forensic accountant at BTG Forensic; Paul Mills, a pensions specialist with BDO Stoy Hayward; Ray Boulger, *the* mortgage guru at brokers John Charcol; Kirsten Gronning, founder of The Divorce Coach; Geeta Varma from the Consumer Credit Counselling Service; James Maguire at law firm DWF; Mary Webber of

Advicenow and Denise Knowles from the relationship advice service, Relate. In all cases, while the expertise is theirs, any mistakes are my own.

I would also like to thank the team at A&C Black, in particular Lisa Carden, who commissioned the book. Lisa's enthusiasm and infectious good humour are much appreciated and her expertise is invaluable. Thanks also to Kate Stenner for editing the book.

At the beginning and end of each chapter I have included a quote from couples who have been through a divorce. Some people I spoke to had experienced a very acrimonious break-up; others were able to end their marriage amicably. Whatever the situation, revisiting your divorce and talking about it is not easy and I am grateful that so many were willing to share their experience.

I am lucky to have friends who have supported me every step of the way; in particular I'd like to mention Dawn Goldsmith who took the time to read several chapters and give me valuable feedback, as well as Caroline Watkin, Sarah Tutt and Linda McCann who offered endless encouragement.

Introduction

Britain has one of the highest divorce rates in Europe and every year around 140,000 couples find themselves facing the prospect of a divorce. There have been many column inches written about why over 40 per cent of marriages break down and why fewer couples are choosing to get married in the first place. But the fact is that the reasons don't really matter to anyone who's going through the break-up of their marriage. Just because many other couples get divorced doesn't mean that you'll find the process any easier.

How you feel about divorce may well come down to whether or not it was your decision. If you feel that your marriage has been on the rocks for some time and have had a number of months or even years to contemplate breaking up, you'll view it very differently from someone who didn't want to split up and for whom the news was a bolt from the blue.

A divorce is about more than splitting up with the person you're married to; the person you imagined you would grow old with. It will also affect any children you have, no matter how amicable you try to keep everything; you may have to sell the home you've shared and you will have to separate finances that have become ever more intertwined over the years. There will be consequences for your family and friends and there will certainly be an impact on your standard of living.

Facing any life-changing experience is difficult. Facing it without the person you thought you were closest to may feel – at times – impossible. You will probably find yourself on a twin track of dealing with emotions that may include grief, anger and hurt and worrying about practical issues around your (and if you have a family, your children's) financial future. On a day-to-day level the emotions may dominate, but the financial consequences of divorce are likely to last for a long time; in some cases, long after the emotional rifts have started to heal.

Understanding what the divorce process involves and the decisions you may have to make will not guarantee a stress-free break-up, but it should give you some control over what you are going through. And that's where this book comes in. It will explain in everyday language what your options are and where the pitfalls lie. You will learn about:

■ which decisions you need to make early in the divorce process and which can wait;

- how your children will be provided for and when you have to involve the CSA;
- the factors that can affect a financial settlement.

You may be rather confused about what financial support you may have to provide for your ex, or what you can expect from him or her. In recent years, London has been christened 'the divorce capital of the world', thanks to a number of high-profile and celebrity divorces. They've grabbed the headlines – at least in part – because of the eye-watering sums of money involved. But for most couples, the process of dividing what they own is very different. Your financial worries may include:

- how you can stretch the money that paid for one household to support two;
- how to minimise the risk of debt problems resulting from your divorce;
- how you can ensure a fair split of what you own without running up massive legal bills.

There have been some changes in recent years that will benefit couples going through a divorce, one of which is an increase in the variety of help that's available. Divorce does not have to involve a legal battle and many family lawyers now offer alternative, less confrontational options. Instead of each side firing off angry letters to each other, your negotiations can be carried out face to face so that all parties knows exactly what's being discussed.

However, while there are some forward-looking developments in terms of the way divorce is handled, the laws that govern divorce and the language that's used are distinctly arcane. This book will explain the legal terms and jargon you're likely to encounter. It will tell you what to expect from the divorce process, what you have to consider at each stage and how you can pay the bills that arise during your divorce. Importantly, it will also help you deal with the emotional fallout of breaking up with your spouse.

There's also a chapter on your rights if you're breaking up with someone you've been living with. Divorce law may be complicated, but at least there are some safeguards if your marriage breaks down. Although couples who live together do have some rights in Scotland, they have very few rights elsewhere in the UK.

The book has been designed so you can dip in and out of it as you need to, or read it in one go so you know exactly what to expect. As well as expert tips and advice, you'll see in each chapter comments from people who are currently going through a divorce or who have recently been divorced. It will give you an insight into what others found difficult and how they dealt with the decisions they had to make.

Knowing what to expect won't mean your divorce is pain-free, but it should reduce the stress. And that will help you to make the right decisions for you and your finances, both now and as you start your life after divorce.

What does divorce mean for us?

STARTING DIVORCE PROCEEDINGS

'My husband said he wanted to move out because he needed some space, but I found out he'd actually been having an affair. I filed for divorce because I wanted to secure my financial situation. We had three young children and the youngest was only two. Naively, I didn't realise that we could make some financial arrangements without the divorce being finalised. I was emotionally punctured by the shock of it all. Friends told me I should fight for myself and the solicitors were quite aggressive as well. As soon as we served the divorce papers on my husband it became incredibly acrimonious and it never recovered.'

The number of marriages that end in divorce has remained stubbornly high for several years, but it's rarely something that couples contemplate lightly. If you're facing divorce, it's because one, or both, of you believes there's no life left in your marriage.

This book sets out to help you deal with the legal and financial consequences of ending a marriage – but it also acknowledges that emotions will have an impact on those consequences. Decisions you take when you are hurt, angry and upset are often very different from the ones you make when you're not.

Where to get emotional support

Although the focus of this book is not on the emotional aspects of divorce, it's useful to know who you can talk to. The relationship counselling service Relate (www.relate. org.uk) deals with marriage and relationship breakdown as well as helping couples stay together. Some people find it easier to talk to someone they don't know about personal matters; others hate the idea of opening up to a stranger. There may be times in the coming months when you feel very lonely, but you are not alone. Don't be afraid to ask for help and support when you need it.

Your friends and family will also be there to give you valuable support, but the advice they give may not always be in your best interests (however well meant it is). They won't want to see you hurt and may think that the best way to help you deal with the pain is by getting back at your ex, or by getting him or her to pay (perhaps literally) for what has happened. That may be something you want as well, but no matter how wronged you have been it's not likely to help you emerge from your divorce any less emotionally bruised.

Relationship counsellors say that there is less emotional scarring from a divorce if both of you can understand why you ended up facing it in the first place. It's not about apportioning blame, but trying to work out what went wrong. Marriage breakdown is rarely 100 per cent one person's 'fault', even if one party is more responsible for what's happened than the other. If you can take steps towards understanding what went wrong, it might – just might – help you cope with the choices you will each face.

Grounds for divorce

One thing that couples either worry about – or feel is unfair – is the fact that the reasons for divorce don't affect the financial outcome (except in *very* rare cases, when one spouse's conduct relating to money might be an issue). However, it's useful to have an understanding of when and why you can get divorced and what the divorce process involves. You may want to get divorced because you no longer love each other or can't live together, but in legal terms there is only one reason (or 'ground') which is that your marriage has broken down irretrievably. If you live in England, Wales or Northern Ireland, you have to be able to show this through one of the following five 'facts'.

1. Adultery: although you don't have to name the person your husband or wife has committed adultery with.
2. Unreasonable behaviour: such that you cannot be expected to live with your husband or wife.
3. Desertion: your husband or wife has 'deserted you' for two years immediately prior to divorce proceedings.
4. Two years' separation with consent: if both parties agree to a divorce.
5. Five years' separation: in which case consent is not needed.

In Scotland, the Family Law Act of 2006 introduced some significant changes to the divorce procedure. It states that couples only have to have been separated for one year (rather than two, as was the case previously) if both partners agree to divorce, and can start divorce proceedings after two years from the date of separation, whether or not both parties agree (rather than the five years in England,

Wales or Northern Ireland). Desertion is also no longer accepted as a 'fact'.

If you live in England or Wales, you cannot get divorced until you have been married for a year, whereas in Scotland there is no minimum waiting period. In Northern Ireland you have to have been married for at least two years before you can start divorce proceedings.

Why 'fault' is still an issue in divorce

It seems strange in the 21st century that, when so many marriages end in divorce, the law (throughout the UK) still insists that one person starts the divorce process and that – in cases where couples want to divorce relatively quickly – one party has to be at 'fault'. In many experts' view, this does nothing to help reduce the stress and hurt of what's often an incredibly painful process.

The way the law stands, unless a couple have lived apart for two years (one year in Scotland) and both want to divorce, they have to allege adultery or unreasonable behaviour in order for the divorce to be granted. That means lawyers have to ask their clients for several examples of unreasonable behaviour as evidence that the marriage has broken down. If you start divorce proceedings, then, the law is encouraging you from the outset to think about the most difficult times during your marriage, while the person you are divorcing will have to read about their alleged behaviour in black and white in the solicitor's letter.

I'll explain more about how to find a solicitor in Chapter 3, but if you use someone who is a member of Resolution (the body that represents solicitors in England and Wales who specialise in divorce), their code of conduct requires them to try and agree the types of unreasonable behaviour with their client before they go any further. My advice is to try – as far as you can – to ignore the concept of fault. At the time it may be difficult, but it's important to realise that it is divorce *law*, rather than your ex, that insists fault is still part of the process in many divorces.

First steps to take

The first steps towards getting divorced are bound to be both emotional and stressful. You will probably be rather overwhelmed by what you are feeling and unsure about what the future holds for you away from your marriage. But it's important that you do not ignore the financial consequences of splitting up, even at this stage. I am not suggesting that you draw up a list of who gets what on day one, rather that you try and understand what decisions you may be faced with and how you and your spouse can deal with them.

There is a world of difference between getting divorced if it's a mutual decision and you can go through the process relatively amicably, and splitting up when it's one partner's idea, especially if there's a lot of anger on both sides. If getting divorced is your idea, you will be in control of the way your husband or wife is given the news. And how you behave may have repercussions on the way the finances are sorted out.

Dos and Don'ts

- Do talk to your husband or wife about why you want a divorce *before* they hear from your lawyer. Don't let the first they know about it be when the solicitor's letter lands on the doormat.
- Do be careful about doing anything in retaliation or to antagonise your husband or wife. You may be angry and upset; you may even want them to suffer, but in the context of divorce proceedings it's unlikely to get you very far.
- Don't worry about how you'll get through the process at this stage. Take one step at a time.
- Don't rush to freeze bank or credit card accounts without giving it serious thought. If you're worried that your partner is about to run up debts, talk to your bank or lender or, if necessary, to your solicitor.
- Do keep an eye on your bank accounts and inform the lenders of your change of circumstances.

■ If you have money problems before you get divorced, these are likely to be made worse by the split. Don't ignore them. Talk to the companies you owe money to as soon as you can.

When moving slowly may not be appropriate

Having warned you of the dangers of rushing into divorce proceedings, there is one exception to the rule; namely if you have been living outside the UK when you *may* be able to get a divorce in that country (or have a choice about whether to divorce there or in the UK). If that's the case, you need to act quickly. This is because once you have started divorce proceedings in one country within the EU, you cannot start them in another. The convention that governs this is called 'Brussels IIA' and there's plenty of information about it on the Internet, if you want to know more.

I'll outline the basic principles here, though. If, for example, you have the choice of getting divorced in England or France and your solicitor advises you that you'd be much better off in financial terms if the divorce took place in England, you should start divorce proceedings there – and the sooner the better. What's important is that you establish that the jurisdictional basis is sound (i.e. that you really do have the right to divorce in that country).

Who can divorce overseas?

Jurisdiction in the EU (including the UK but with the exception of Denmark) can be based on the fact that you have lived in the particular country for at least one year, or at least six months if you are returning to your permanent home (in the UK) or to the country of your nationality (for the rest of the EU except Denmark). Alternatively, if you want to get divorced in the UK, jurisdiction is based on where you and your spouse are domiciled – where your permanent home is, in other words. You can leave one country and become domiciled in another, but you would have to prove that you had permanently or indefinitely settled there. It wouldn't be enough for you to have lived there for a period of time.

For the other EU states (except Denmark!), jurisdiction is based on the nationality of both spouses. Under the rules of Brussels IIA, if you were either resident or domiciled (for the UK) or resident in or national of another EU country, you would be able to apply to divorce there. Within the EU, the rule to claim divorce jurisdiction is 'first past the post'. That means that the country in which you first start divorce action (as long as you meet qualification criteria) is where the divorce will take place.

The EU is taking steps to harmonise the way financial settlements in divorce are treated through a paper called 'Rome III'. It would mean that the UK would have to have a similar approach to working out how much maintenance should be paid (to a spouse) as elsewhere in the EU. The UK made a decision at the end of 2006 not to opt in to Rome III and remains opted out at the time of writing, although that could change at a later date.

If you have the choice of getting divorced in the UK or the United States (or another non-EU country), the Brussels IIA convention doesn't apply. Instead, a court hearing would decide in which country the divorce should take place (although the court would take into account where the divorce proceedings were started). It may also look at other factors, such as where you have lived as a couple and where your assets are located.

Divorcing overseas may be advantageous to the financially stronger party (normally, but not always, the husband). That's because in many countries, couples are not under the same obligation to disclose all their assets and the financially weaker party is not normally entitled to ongoing maintenance. However, the situation does vary between countries and is something you would need to take expert legal advice on.

> Where you get divorced affects far more than the amount of maintenance you may receive or be asked to pay. For example, while pre-nuptial agreements are not legally recognised in England, Wales and Northern Ireland (although this is being reviewed and currently their contents may be taken into account by the courts), they have full legal status in many other countries.

What your solicitor will do:

1   find out whether you have a choice of countries you could get divorced in;
2   advise you on the possible outcome of getting divorced in the UK
    (depending on where in the UK you live);
3   establish how this compares with the other country you may be able to
    get divorced in (which normally involves contacting lawyers in those
    countries directly).

Checking out your legal rights

When you first think about getting divorced, you will probably want to do your own research to find out what the future may hold. The Internet is a great source of information, but be aware that you won't always know how accurate the articles and comments are and who is behind the website address. And they may have a vested interest in emphasising a particular aspect. If you type 'divorce' or 'legal process' and 'money' into Google, you'll get dozens of different sites that offer to guide you through the basics.

Some of the content is very basic indeed, so you may have to glue yourself to your PC for a few hours to track down what you need. If you want more detailed information on DIY online divorce and other websites that may help, you'll find it in Chapter 3, along with advice on how to find a lawyer.

What divorce may mean for your finances

Wherever you get divorced, there is no doubt that the break-up of your marriage is likely to have a significant effect on your finances. It seems so obvious that you might think it doesn't need spelling out. But while you might be able to accept the *idea* that there will be less money to go round post-divorce, it can be a very different matter when you have to try and deal with the practical implications of no longer being married to the main wage earner, or have to move out of the family home and try to buy somewhere else. However, accepting that divorce will mean you have less money – possibly a lot less – is one of the most important steps along the way.

Debt counsellors tell me that many of the people who come to them for help do so because their marriage or long-term relationship has broken down. There are cases where the debts have been run up by one person but were taken out in both parties' names, but there are many other examples where one or both parties has not been realistic about how much they have to live on.

It can be difficult if you see your ex enjoying a certain standard of living (perhaps because they have a new partner or because they're in a well paid job). The temptation is to think that you deserve a similar standard of living, but if trying to match your ex's spending means taking on more debt (and especially if it means taking on more debt than you can afford to repay), it isn't the answer.

In order to keep your spending and borrowing under control, you have to brace yourself for a new life with less money than you've been used to. Depending on the circumstances leading up to your divorce, you may feel that's a small price to pay for getting your life back.

Relationship counsellors say that the person who drives the divorce is often more prepared to make the necessary financial sacrifices than the other, as they can see that there's a 'trade-off'. What is very hard is for the person who is not in control of the divorce process to accept is that their standard of living will also suffer as a result – and sometimes more than their ex-husband or wife's.

> Some divorcing parents try to compensate their children for the stress of the marriage breakdown by buying presents and expensive trips. Be careful about going down this route. If your children are very young, they probably won't understand what's going on and won't really appreciate why they're being given more presents and treats than usual. If they're older, they may realise why they're being spoiled and it could upset them if they think they are being 'bought off'. Alternatively, they may try to play their super-generous parents for all they are worth, to extract the maximum amount of 'financial compensation' possible!

How will your assets be divided?

Divorce lawyers are often asked in the early days how much someone may receive or have to give up when they get divorced. It's quite difficult for them to give a direct answer as cases vary (except in Scotland, where the guidelines are more closely adhered to), but there are basic principles that govern the way your home, money, savings, pensions and other assets you own could be divided.

If you have children, the first priority will be to make sure that they are provided for. After that, the aim is to allow the husband and wife enough to pay for their needs (such as housing etc.). Once needs have been catered for, any money and property that's left and that you've both acquired during your marriage will be divided. If one of you is relatively wealthy compared to the other, it is quite likely that some of the assets you own will be transferred to your spouse.

If you have no idea how much you're worth between you or how the family finances are run, you should try and get up to speed – and quickly. Often in a relationship, one partner will make more of the day-to-day financial decisions than the other. If one of you has always been a much higher earner than the other, he or she may have taken it upon themselves to make decisions about how 'their' money is invested. Conversely, they may have put the investments in the name of the lower earner, to reduce tax. Whatever your circumstances, it's vital that you get an accurate picture of your financial worth as a couple.

If you cannot agree how the assets should be divided, it will be down to the courts to decide, so a divorce lawyer will always give you advice based on what the courts would do. However, in England and Wales, they have a fair amount of discretion about how a financial settlement is achieved. The rules are rather different in Scotland and slightly different in Northern Ireland, so I'll explain what happens in each country later on.

In England and Wales, divorcing couples have to disclose their assets and debts in a document called 'form E'. It's quite a lengthy form (around 25 pages) which asks questions about everything from the value of your property and any mortgage secured on it to how much you owe in credit card debts and bank loans. You also have to give information about how much money you require for yourself and your children (if you're making a request for what is called 'ancillary relief', i.e. maintenance for your children, yourself and/or transfer of assets). Some people I spoke to found the form hard to fill in, not because the questions are particularly difficult, but because it was hard to concentrate on financial matters at such an emotional time. You can get a copy from the HM Courts website (www.hmcourts-service.gov.uk).

What the courts take into account

While the courts take certain factors into account, it doesn't mean that they will necessarily come up with a particular solution (except in Scotland). There may be two or three different options that would achieve the same outcome. If you and your husband or wife had a preference for one way of dividing up the assets, the courts would certainly listen to what you wanted. The factors the courts take into account include:

- how long you have been married;
- how old you and your husband or wife are;
- how healthy you are (if you are not in a position to work and support yourself, that would affect how your joint wealth was divided);
- the earning capacity of each of you;
- your standard of living while you were married;
- the contribution that each of you made to the family;
- how much money each of you needs and what your financial commitments are;
- how much you would give up as a result of the financial settlement. For example, if you had to share your pension with your ex, that would reduce your own pension.

How assets are divided in Scotland

The situation in Scotland is different from that in England, Wales and Northern Ireland. What's important here is not the date at which you divorced, but the date of separation. As far as the courts are concerned, property, money or other assets that you or your spouse bought, inherited or acquired either before you married or after the date of separation are largely irrelevant.

The courts in Scotland will usually divide everything built up during marriage equally, but can deviate from that in some circumstances. To do so, they will look at various factors (some of which will also form the basis for deciding if there should be any support paid after divorce). They include:

- whether one party suffered economic disadvantage from being married or bringing up children, or if one party gained an economic advantage from the contributions of the other;
- who has the economic burden of caring for children under the age of 16 and making sure that is shared fairly by both parties;
- whether provision needs to be made to offset the effects of serious financial hardship that will result from divorce;
- whether one party has been dependent to a substantial degree on financial support from the other.

Scotland favours clean break settlements and it is unusual for there to be any support paid after divorce. But if it is to be paid, it must be for at least one of three reasons:

1 because the economic burden of childcare needs to be shared equally;
2 because one party has been dependent to a substantial degree on the other;
3 because one party is likely to suffer serious financial hardship as a result of divorce.

Just because one or more of these factors exists does not mean that support, called 'periodic allowance', will be paid. The court can only make an award for periodic allowance in Scotland if it is satisfied that an order for capital would be inappropriate or insufficient. In most cases it's paid on the basis that one party has been substantially dependent on the other, in which case it can only be paid for up to three years from divorce to enable them to look for work and, if necessary, retrain.

Although the Scottish courts only take account of 'matrimonial property', which is money and assets that have been acquired by the couple after they married (and before they separated), there are exceptions. If a house or flat was bought before the couple got married and was intended for them to live in as a family home, it is matrimonial property, while anything inherited or received as a gift from someone other than the couple during the marriage is not matrimonial property. If pensions and endowments were started before the marriage, the proportion that relates to the period before marriage is also not matrimonial property.

MATRIMONIAL PROPERTY

'My husband had his own business, so when he told me he wanted a divorce, I assumed that I'd be entitled to some of it, especially as I'd supported him while he was building up the business. My lawyer started looking at the accounts to work out how much it was worth, but one day he told me I wasn't entitled to any of it because my husband had actually formed the company before we were married. Even though it hadn't traded until after we were married, under Scottish law, it wasn't something I was entitled to a share of.'

First steps in the divorce process

How will you pay for your divorce?

It may seem odd to talk about how you will pay for your divorce this early in the book. Surely there are more important things to worry about, like where you will live and how you will manage once you are divorced? Well in the longer term, definitely. But if you cannot pay for the divorce, or you're forced to make a financial settlement because your soon-to-be ex knows money is tight, it could have longer-term implications.

There are different types of costs associated with divorce. If you are filing for divorce on the basis of unreasonable behaviour or adultery, you may ask your spouse to pay the costs of the divorce itself. If the break-up is amicable, there's no reason why you shouldn't split the costs. Costs for other issues, such as negotiating a financial settlement, are dealt with separately and these are the ones that can become expensive.

Paying legal costs can be a struggle for anyone, but if you're going through a divorce it can be even harder. That's especially true if you have little money of your own, perhaps because you have given up work to care for the children. So it's worth taking some time to look at what your options are during the divorce process, how you can raise money to pay the legal bills until the financial settlement is finalised and whether you are eligible for Legal Aid.

Cash-raising options

- 0 per cent credit card
- credit card cheques
- bank loan
- matrimonial costs loan
- Legal Aid

0 per cent credit card

If you can get a credit card that charges 0 per cent on purchases (especially if the deal runs for quite a long time – say a year or more), you could use it to pay your legal bills. Once the 0 per cent deal runs out the interest rate can rise quite sharply, but it might give you the breathing space you need. I found several credit cards with 0 per cent deals lasting for six months or more by looking at a number of price comparison websites. I won't list the sites here as I've covered them in more detail on pp. 144–5 in Chapter 8. Most solicitors accept payment by credit card, but it's worth checking when you first speak to yours.

Credit card cheques

This is a difficult one. I don't like credit card cheques because I think they encourage people to take on unnecessary debt and they're an expensive way of borrowing. That's because interest is charged on day one, just as it is when you use your credit card to take out cash. On top of that they don't give you the same consumer protection that using your credit card offers. Having said this, if you're really up against it financially but you *know* your situation will improve in the not-too-distant future, they may be worth considering if you don't have another option.

Bank loan

If you can't find a 0 per cent credit card, try for a low interest rate loan. Your bank may offer you a preferential rate if you're an existing customer (but don't count on it!), otherwise shop around for a competitive deal. Be aware that the interest rate that's quoted on websites or adverts may not necessarily be the rate you are offered. Increasingly, loan providers work out how much interest they'll charge on the basis of your credit report and factors like employment status.

> Don't take on extra credit if you're already in a financial black hole. What a 0 per cent credit card or bank loan should enable you to do is pay the bills (including legal costs) until your financial situation improves. However, if you know that's unlikely to happen once the divorce has been finalised, try not to borrow more from the bank or credit card companies. If you can't keep up the repayments, you'll have bigger money problems than you started out with.

Matrimonial costs loan

A few financial companies have specific products (called a matrimonial costs loan, matrimonial fee funding or a matrimonial dispute loan) designed to help with legal costs. Some banks, especially those that target wealthy customers, have wised up to the fact that an increasing number of their clients are likely to get a divorce at some point in their lives. More importantly – from the bank's point of view – a number of them will receive a sizeable lump sum as part of their settlement. So, as a condition of getting the loan, you may be asked to let the bank invest your lump sum for you, which I'm not convinced is a good deal. However, if you do go down this route, find out how long you would be tied to the bank for, how much it charges for managing your money and – crucially – how well money it has invested for other clients has performed. Companies that offer matrimonial loans include Butterfield Bank (www. butterfieldprivatebank.co.uk), HSBC Private Bank (www. hsbcprivatebank.com) and Coutts (www.coutts.com). Not all insist on management of any lump sum you receive.

Heritable Bank has a slightly different product, which is aimed at divorce lawyers rather than people going through a divorce. It gives solicitors the chance to offer their clients up to three years' credit, but only if they think the client is likely to receive a financial settlement that means they will be able to repay the loan.

While the divorce is ongoing, you only have to pay the interest every month (which, at the time of writing, works out at around £13.30 on a loan of £1,500). At the end of the loan period, or when you receive your financial settlement, you have to repay the original lump sum you borrowed. If, for any reason, you were unable to repay, your solicitor would have to pay it on your behalf. There is more information at www.heritable.co.uk.

In Scotland, banks do not generally offer matrimonial costs or fees loans. However many solicitors recognise that paying legal bills can be a problem and so may defer the majority of their fees. A typical scenario would be where you would pay the VAT, plus any fees the solicitor incurs (such as accountants' fees etc.) at the time, but would be able to settle the solicitor's own fees at a later date.

Legal Aid

If you can't afford a solicitor, you may be able to get help through Legal Aid, which is operated through Community Legal Advice (www.communitylegaladvice.org.uk). The terminology for Legal Aid has been through several changes and the criteria for eligibility seem to change quite regularly as well. At the time of writing, you would not qualify for Legal Aid if:

- your gross salary (before income tax and National Insurance have been deducted) is more than £2,530 (2008–2009) in the last month, although there is a higher limit if you have more than four children;
- you have more than £8,000 in 'disposable capital'. Disposable capital includes savings, shares, property (including your main home), assets held in trust and money linked to your business. However, if the property has a mortgage and/or loan secured on it, this is taken off the property's value (up to a maximum mortgage of £100,000). If it's your main home, a further £100,000 of its value is ignored. The value of cars (unless they are not in everyday use), household furniture and clothing are not taken into account.

If your income is below £2,530 a month you should deduct income tax, National Insurance, childcare costs (incurred due to work), maintenance payments, housing costs and set allowances for your spouse and dependent children living with you. If you have more than £698 a month disposable income, you will still not qualify for Legal Aid.

If you are eligible, there are different types of Legal Aid assistance.

- Advice and assistance with undefended divorce is available through Legal Help.

- Legal representation may be available in limited circumstances for a defended divorce or (in exceptional cases) where you would be unable to proceed without representation, for an uncontested divorce.
- Financial matters are funded through Family Help. This covers financial negotiations and formalising a settlement.
- If the financial settlement cannot be agreed through negotiations, Legal Representation may be available.

You can get further information from the Community Legal Advice website. It includes a calculator to help you work out what help you might get. It is available at: www.communitylegaladvice.org.uk/en/legalaid/calculator.jsp.

If you do get help with legal costs, you may still have to make a contribution to your legal fees, either as a lump sum (called 'capital contribution') or by monthly instalments (called 'income contribution'). However, you would not be required to pay anything towards legal costs if you have less than £301 a month in disposable income, or if your capital is below £3,000.

Statutory charge

Whether or not you have to make monthly contributions, you may be asked to pay back your legal funding from any money or assets (such as the house) that you receive through what's called a 'statutory charge'. In a divorce case, the costs would include those relating to the divorce itself, financial and children issues (plus domestic violence or other injunctions).

If, for example, you were awarded a lump sum, you would have to repay Legal Aid costs straight away, unless you used it to buy a home (in which case you would still need to be able to demonstrate that you would be at risk of losing your home by paying back the legal costs immediately). If you were able to keep your home as a result of the divorce case, or had gained a greater share in it, you might not have to pay the money back immediately. Instead, you could have a charge registered against it, which you would have to pay back once the property was sold.

If you could not repay legal costs straight away, you may be able to pay them in instalments. In this case, a legal (or statutory) charge would remain on your house until the last instalment was paid off. With a statutory charge, you pay 'simple' interest at 8 per cent. On most loans, while you do not make any payments, interest is 'rolled up', so you are charged interest on the unpaid interest that has accrued (which makes the loan more expensive). In this case interest is not added to unpaid interest, so on a £5,000 charge, you'd pay £400 interest a year.

There are separate, but similar schemes for Legal Aid in Scotland and Northern Ireland. In Northern Ireland, Legal Aid is much more readily available for a divorce than it is in England and Wales, but not for reaching a financial settlement. Contact the Scottish Legal Aid Board (www.slab.org.uk) or the Northern Ireland Legal Services Commission (www.nilsc.org.uk) for more information.

Financial steps to take

Once you've sorted out how you will pay for your divorce, you should turn your attention to other financial areas. You may feel overwhelmed by the stress of divorce and worried about how you will manage financially. My advice is not to bury your head in the sand. If your ex has traditionally paid some or most of the bills, try to have a conversation about how they will be paid in the future. I'm not talking about what happens in the long term; that can be sorted out later. What you should clarify is who will pay important bills while you try to work out your divorce.

To do:

■ Work out what you spend at the moment and what you have coming in by drawing up a simple budget. You can find a budget calculator on the

Financial Services Authority's website at www.moneymadeclear.fsa.
gov.uk.

- Make a list of outgoings and who is currently responsible for them.
  Try to agree who will pay for what.
- If you need to contact phone companies, energy suppliers etc. to tell
  them that you are taking over the bill, do it as soon as you can.
- Make sure the mortgage or rent is paid.
- Talk to your bank if you think you may need to take out an overdraft or
  borrow more. Don't go overdrawn without their permission as you may
  be hit with hefty charges.

There are more details on how to deal with money-
related issues in Chapter 8.

The family home: who stays?

Unless your divorce is very amicable (or finances are
particularly tight), one of you will probably want to move
out of the family home. If you own it between you, your
position will be protected in law, whether or not you've
moved out. The overriding concern may be a practical one.
If your ex is particularly antagonistic, he or she may decide
to change the locks and throw all your possessions into the
nearest skip the moment you're out of the front door. If
you can't stay with family or friends until you find
somewhere to live, you may have to remain in your home
while you look for a flat or house you can rent. There are

more details about this in Chapter 5, but it might be worth taking action sooner rather than later.

> If the family home is owned jointly, you each automatically have a say in what happens. It doesn't necessarily mean that the proceeds will be divided equally when you get divorced, but it does mean that one partner cannot sell the property without the other's permission. If your husband or wife owns your home outright and you are worried that he or she will go for a quick sale, you can ask a solicitor to register a 'matrimonial home rights notice' (called an 'inhibition' in Scotland) against it. It's a charge that will appear on the Land Register and will protect your position.

What to expect from the divorce process

England and Wales

High profile divorce cases create the headlines because they involve a court appearance. But the reality is that 90 per cent of divorces don't get to that stage; instead they are completed on paper. I'll give you details on the process in England and Wales first and will highlight any differences in Scotland and Northern Ireland afterwards. If you want to find out more, visit the Courts Service website (www.hmcourts-service.gov.uk). I'll also mention leaflets, forms and guidance notes that I think are particularly useful.

Steps along the way

- The person who starts divorce proceedings is called the 'petitioner' while the person they are divorcing is called the 'respondent'. If you're getting divorced because of your husband or wife's adultery, it's generally better not to name the third party as it often leads to acrimony. However, if you choose to identify them, their legal title is 'co-respondent'.
- Assuming you (rather than your spouse) start divorce proceedings, you will need to get hold of a form called a 'petition'. If you're using a lawyer, he or she will fill it in for you. If you're not, you can download one from the Courts Service website yourself. The petition is called form D8 and comes with notes for guidance on how to fill it in. I'd also recommend that you read form D184, which sets out in very straightforward terms which forms you have to fill in, what you may have to pay to file them (if you're going down the DIY route) and what happens once you've sent your forms off.

  Don't worry about the off-putting language. The petition talks about the 'prayer' (which simply means what you're asking the courts to do – namely to grant a divorce) and the 'facts' of divorce. Your lawyer will explain any jargon to you and the guidance notes on the Courts Service website are user-friendly and easy to follow.

You will have to give details about why you are asking for a divorce, both in terms of which 'fact' you are citing and what has actually happened (for example, the date on which your husband or wife moved out, if you are divorcing after you have separated). You also have to spell out whether you are asking for financial support for yourself and/or your children. It's usual to include all claims for financial relief (otherwise called ancillary relief) in the petition in case you want to pursue them later on.

You will need a copy of your marriage certificate, which you can get from the General Register Office (www.gro.gov.uk). You have to pay a fee to file the divorce petition, which is currently £300, while the fee for filing an answer (a defence to the petition) is £210. If you're petitioning for divorce, you will also have to swear an affidavit (which can cost around £7.50) and pay £40 to get the decree absolute. You have to pay court fees by cheque, postal order or cash. Credit and debit cards are not accepted.

- If you're on a low income or claiming benefits, such as income support, income-based jobseeker's allowance, state pension guarantee credit or working tax credit (but with no child tax credit), you should not have to pay the court fee.

There is a form EX160A (called 'Court fees – Do I have to pay them?') which you can download from the Courts Service website, or pick up from any county court. Even if you are not entitled to complete exemption from paying court fees, you may be able to pay a reduced amount. However, you have to apply separately for exemption from each fee.

- Once you or your lawyer has sent in the petition (or taken them in person) to the court, you will receive another form (D9H) that tells you the petition has been sent to your husband or wife. The courts will also provide you with a receipt for any fee you have paid and a divorce case number.

- If you have children, you will also have to send off a 'statement of arrangements'. Here you are asked for information relating to where the children currently live, who cares for them, whether any maintenance is being paid at the moment and, if not, whether you are applying for maintenance, along with details for contact between your children and your ex. You should have three copies of every form you fill in; a copy for yourself, one for the courts and one for your ex.

- The court will post your form with an acknowledgement of service, form D10, which your husband or wife has to fill in to show they've received the petition. They then have eight days from the day after they receive the petition to return the acknowledgement.

- If your husband or wife does not return the acknowledgement of service, it could be because you don't have the correct address or – more likely – because they don't want to co-operate. If it's the latter, you can ask court bailiffs to serve the petition on your spouse. However, family lawyers tell me that the court bailiff service is not always very efficient, so you may be better off using what's called a 'private process server'. They will charge an hourly rate (which can vary widely, but may be around £50) to serve the petition. Alternatively, if your ex tells you they have the petition but have no intention of filing an acknowledgement, you can swear an affidavit saying that. It's normally seen as sufficient evidence of service.

- You need to swear a short standard form affidavit exhibiting the acknowledgement of service form and send that to the court. The district judge then considers the divorce petition and any arrangements for the children. Once the judge is satisfied, he or she will list a decree nisi hearing. It may take several weeks – or even longer – for the hearing to take place, but there's no need for either of you to attend the court in person.

- Six weeks and one day after the decree nisi has been granted, the petitioner can apply for a decree absolute, which finalises the divorce. If the petitioner hasn't applied for a decree absolute within three months of the decree nisi, the respondent is able to.

Most divorces are undefended, but some are not. In a number of cases, a spouse who's had an affair has been able to petition for divorce first on the basis of unreasonable behaviour. The obvious answer is to counter-petition, but it can be an expensive business. Whether it's important enough to outweigh the costs will be down to you.

No court order can be made to regulate financial issues before the decree nisi, even if you've sorted everything out amicably and only need a consent order to turn it into a legally binding agreement. However, you can still sort out financial matters after the divorce has been finalised and there's no time limit by which the courts have to make orders in relation to financial settlements. The only time you would lose your right to apply to the courts in relation to finances is if you remarry.

Date of separation

There may be quite some time between the date that you and your spouse separate and when you start divorce proceedings, but the timing is important. The date of separation is the date you physically separate from your spouse. You and your ex may have been living 'separate lives' in the same home for some months or even years and it may be that this can count towards separation, but only if you have lived entirely separately and, for example, have not cooked for each other or shared time together. This date is relevant if you are planning a divorce on the grounds of separation.

It also has tax and financial implications. For example, husbands and wives are not liable for capital gains tax on any property or assets that are transferred between them from the date of separation until the end of the tax year. So, if you and your spouse separate on 6 April, you'll have until 5 April the following year to transfer assets etc. without incurring capital gains tax liability. However, if the date of separation is 4 April, you would only have one day in which to sort it out. It may be hard to tie an emotional decision to a tax calendar, but you could be left with additional costs to pay if you don't manage it. There are special exemptions relating to the former matrimonial home, which I'll explain in Chapter 5.

Drawing up a separation agreement

When you separate, it's a good idea to draw up an agreement that states what will happen in relation to any children you have and your finances. It might include details of how much child support and/or maintenance will be paid by one to the other, who will pay the mortgage and whether the family home is to be sold now or on divorce. If the two of you cannot agree the terms of the agreement, you may have to get help from your solicitor. You'll also need one to turn it into a legally binding 'deed of separation'.

Divorce process in Scotland

There are significant differences to the divorce process in Scotland compared to England and Wales. One of the most obvious is the fact that you can start proceedings at any point after marriage if you are divorcing your spouse on the grounds of unreasonable behaviour or adultery. If you want to make use of financial protective orders, which are designed to stop your spouse from selling their assets or property or from hiding assets, you may choose to raise an action on the grounds of unreasonable behaviour so that you can tell the court about your spouse's conduct. You might also cite unreasonable behaviour as a reason for divorce if, for example, your spouse had a drugs or gambling habit which resulted in them selling off some of your joint possessions. It is very unusual for one spouse's behaviour to affect the financial settlement, but in this case it would be relevant.

The vast majority of marriages end with a divorce granted after a period of separation: either one year, with the consent of the other spouse, or two years, which doesn't need their consent. Only a relatively small minority of divorces are the result of unreasonable behaviour or adultery. The divorce decree doesn't specify the basis on which the divorce was granted.

Where to divorce

You have two options when it comes to where you get divorced in Scotland:

- the Sheriff Court
- the Court of Session

Scotland is currently undergoing a review of the structure of its civil courts. It means that in future, all divorces could be heard at the Sheriff Court, but at the time of writing, the review has some way go. It's worth checking with your solicitor to see whether the situation has changed or is likely to change in the near future.

The Sheriff Court

Where you live may have some bearing on the type of court you use for your divorce. The Sheriff Court is a local court and in Scotland, unlike in England and Wales, you can only apply to your local court to hear your case. You also have to have lived in the Sheriffdom for at least 40 days to do so. While there are several Sheriff Courts, there is only one Court of Session, which is based in Edinburgh.

Aside from location, the main advantage of raising your divorce action in the Sheriff Court is that you don't have to use a solicitor advocate (the Scottish equivalent of a barrister) or counsel. You *can* still use counsel in the Sheriff Court if you want to, and this often happens when cases are complicated or unusual.

However, there are disadvantages to using this court, the main one being that orders from the Sheriff Court are harder to enforce elsewhere in the UK or overseas than those from the Court of Session. So if you think you will have to enforce an order outside Scotland, you may be better off getting your divorce heard in the Court of Session.

The Court of Session

In some divorce cases, such as those involving parties who don't live in Scotland, you can only raise your divorce action in the Court of Session. If you do so, you have to instruct a solicitor advocate or counsel. But as many solicitor advocates don't do family cases, you would probably end up instructing counsel. This would add to your costs as you'll have to pay both a solicitor and counsel. The Court of Session is typically used for 'big money' divorces, those that are complex and those where there is an international (or English) dimension. The questions you should ask yourself when you're deciding whether to raise the action for divorce in the Court of Session or Sheriff Court are:

- Do you live near the Court of Session?
- How complex is your divorce likely to be?
- How much money is involved?
- How long do you think it might take (divorces raised in the Court of Session often take longer than those raised in the Sheriff Court)?
- Will you have to enforce orders overseas or in England?

International divorces and Scotland

If there's any potential of you having to raise action for divorce in Scotland or elsewhere in the UK, you must make sure you get advice about where to get divorced. The country you end up getting divorced in will depend on where you last lived together. In practice, this means you can raise an action for divorce in Scotland and, for example, start divorce proceedings in England and then work out where you will actually divorce. Starting divorce proceedings in one country does not mean you cannot do so elsewhere.

However, if you start divorce proceedings in another EU country (except Denmark) and also in Scotland, you can only continue with them in the country where the divorce action was initially raised. It doesn't mean, though, that you then have to proceed with the divorce at a breakneck speed, as it is possible to freeze the action (it's called 'sisting', in legal language) while you negotiate the financial terms of the split.

Key stages in the divorce process in Scotland

In the vast majority of cases in Scotland, it would be very unusual to raise a divorce action without entering into negotiations first. There is no equivalent of the form E that's used in England and Wales, but once you've separated, your solicitor will help you identify the matrimonial property. When you go and see him or her you will be asked for details of the assets and liabilities that you had at the date you separated (called the 'relevant date').

It's useful if you can also provide a list of where those assets came from. Were they bought with money you acquired, with money of both of you had or were they the result of an inheritance or gift? Some people will have a clear idea of what they own and where the money comes from; others will not. Because the courts in Scotland have less freedom to deviate from the guidelines than they do in England and Wales, it is easier for solicitors in Scotland to give advice about the possible financial settlement at an early stage.

The end result of the financial side of the separation, once the courts have decided how they want to divide up the assets and liabilities, is the 'Minute of Agreement' (sometimes called a 'Separation Agreement'), which is a binding legal contract. Once it has been drawn up, the courts will not then review it. This is very different from the system that operates in England and Wales, where the courts might review an agreement at any time.

Just because you have a Minute of Agreement does not mean that you and your spouse have to go on to get divorced. Many couples separate and draw up a Minute of Agreement, but do not get divorced as it can be enforced in the same way as a court order.

DIY divorce in Scotland

If you and your spouse have a Minute of Agreement in place (or if you don't want to seek any financial orders from each other) and don't have children under the age of 16, you can then use the simplified (or DIY) divorce procedure which is much cheaper and quicker than the standard procedure. You can download the forms you need from the Internet and get a divorce for £70. A DIY divorce, however, is only suitable for couples who meet the following criteria:

1   You need to be able to satisfy the jurisdiction grounds, which normally mean that you must have lived in Scotland for at least six months before you apply for a divorce. There are several ways to satisfy the jurisdiction grounds and more information is available at www.scotcourts.gov.uk.

2   You must have no children under the age of 16.

3   You must not make a financial claim against your spouse and vice versa.

4   There cannot be any other court proceedings.

5   You must have lived apart for one year and have consent for divorce in
     writing, or for two years if you do not have written consent.

A simplified divorce may seem like a good idea, but there are drawbacks: you would not be able to make any financial claims at a later date. As there is no decree nisi/absolute system in Scotland, once you are divorced you lose the right to make any claims.

Divorce process in Northern Ireland

Although there are many similarities between the divorce system in Northern Ireland and that in England and Wales, there are some significant differences. One is that the petitioner has to give evidence, in person, in front of a judge as part of the divorce process. You can either get divorced in the county court or the High Court, but if your divorce is defended, only the High Court can deal with it. It also tends to deal with 'big money' divorce cases. The advantage is that the High Court hears divorce cases every day, so yours is likely to be finalised more quickly, but the fees it charges for petitioning for divorce are higher than the county court. However, unless you live in or near Belfast, it will be much more convenient to have your divorce hearing in a county court.

As with elsewhere in the UK, you don't have to use a solicitor. You can contact the Northern Ireland Court Service (www.courtsni.gov.uk) and inform them that you want to petition for a divorce as a personal petitioner.

A divorce action is launched when the petitioner sends a petition to the courts (along with a statement of arrangements and court fees). Once the respondent returns the acknowledgement of service, the petitioner is able to lodge a 'Certificate of Readiness' with the Court (which costs around £300 for the High Court and £250 for a county court). Once that's happened, you'll get a notification of a date for the hearing from the court. If you have reached agreement on the finances, it's normally handed to the Master (a junior judge) at the same time. If you're on Legal Aid, you cannot start financial negotiations until the decree nisi has been granted. If you are fee-paying, you can.

The starting point for financial negotiations is full disclosure of your financial situation. In the majority of cases, agreement is through negotiation, but if you cannot agree on how assets should be split, you will have to attend a hearing in front of a Master. Most people prefer to go for a clean break settlement, although spousal maintenance may be paid if one party needs help to get back into employment or, in big money cases, if there is financial inequality.

SORTING OUT THE FINANCES YOURSELF

'Although my wife had an affair while we were married, the decision to divorce was mutual. We'd been separated for a couple of years when I met someone else. That's what prompted me to start divorce proceedings. It was all very straightforward because the dust had settled and we could talk about money quite calmly. We'd never had joint accounts, we'd both worked throughout our marriage and there were no children – so no child maintenance to sort out. We agreed how we'd divide everything between us; the proceeds of the house would be split 50:50 and my ex-wife said she wasn't interested in my pension.'

Getting professional help

A LEGAL CHALLENGE

'I used a law firm that someone at work had mentioned, but whenever I wanted to speak to my solicitor, he was never there and he hardly ever returned my calls. After a couple of months, someone else took on my case and then she went on maternity leave, so a third solicitor took over. I felt there was a real change in attitude from the firm once I'd instructed them. If I went through it all again, I'd ask many more questions before I signed up with someone.'

What help is available?

When you think about divorce, one image that might spring to mind is of solicitors' bills – and probably large ones at that. But you don't have to spend a lot of money to get divorced, and may not even have to use a solicitor. If you want to pay for professional help, there's a wide range of expertise available, from specialist divorce lawyers (otherwise known as 'family lawyers') to trained mediators who will help you and your ex to reach a solution with the minimal involvement of lawyers, and online divorce sites. And that's without including counsellors and relationship advisers who are there specifically to help you cope with the emotional side of the process. It's up to you how much professional help you use (if you decide to use any at all) and who you use. This chapter will explain exactly what's on offer, how much it could cost and how to get the best out of the professionals you employ.

Online divorce and information sites

If the Internet is your starting point, you'll find a mind-boggling number of websites that are designed to offer legal advice, explain the basics of the process or just give you a chance to talk to others who are in a similar situation. Some sites are useful and have up-to-date information, others are less so and may not.

There are also quite a few websites offering a cut-price divorce service. As well as promising to save money, they appeal to people who like the idea of being able to sort everything out from the comfort of their home (or desk). Prices start at around £65 for the most basic service, rising to £300 or more for a comprehensive divorce package. However, they're only suitable for divorces that are amicable and uncontested as they cannot deal with any dispute. The more straightforward your situation (for example, if you have only been married for a short time and you have enough capital to split between you relatively easily), the better it is.

When you're looking for an online divorce service check:

- whether it offers help with filling in forms or fills them in for you;
- whether it has professional indemnity insurance in case you need to make a claim against it;
- whether you will be offered a consent (or clean break) order to finalise your settlement, which means that your ex won't be able to bring any claim against you in the future. (Some websites only offer this on more expensive services.)

This is a real growth area and new online divorce services are springing up all the time. Bear in mind that divorce sites which are around as I'm writing this book may have changed or disappeared by the time you're reading it! They may have been taken over by rivals, merged or had a revamp of their content.

Here are some websites to try:

- **WWW.FILE4DIVORCE.CO.UK.** This offers a fixed-fee divorce service, but it also has a lot of information which you can access for free. All divorces are handled by solicitors (rather than paralegals, who are only qualified to carry out legal administrative work) and a fixed-fee divorce costs £400, with additional charges for negotiating a financial settlement. What I like about the site is that you can get your divorce question answered online for free, and view and search questions and answers already submitted by other users. You can also telephone a freephone number for further no-obligation advice from a solicitor if your situation is too complicated to be dealt with via email.

- **WWW.DIVORCE-ONLINE.CO.UK.** This site was set up in 1999 and has dealt with tens of thousands of divorces. Its DIY service costs £65 plus VAT, which means all the documents are prepared and filed at local courts, and you can email or ring a national rate number for help. Most customers, though, choose to spend more for its solicitor-managed service (which costs £320 plus VAT). All forms are prepared by a qualified solicitor and letters, emails and legal advice are included. The cheapest options do not include a consent order, which has to be bought separately.

- **WWW.QUICKEDIVORCE.CO.UK.** This online divorce site is owned by divorce-online. Prices are a little cheaper and it includes a useful frequently asked questions section.

- **WWW.INSIDEDIVORCE.COM.** This site doesn't offer a DIY divorce service, but has a range of information and articles for people contemplating or going through divorce. You can browse articles and the forum for free, although you have to register (which is also free) if you want to post a message. Some of the information was useful, but in my view there has been rather a motley assortment of articles when I've visited the site.

- **WWW.MANAGED-DIVORCE.CO.UK.** This site offers a range of online divorce services with prices from £167 to £397. I have to confess to finding the rest of the website a bit of a puzzle; at the time of writing it included a resources page which carries an advert for an introduction service where you can provide companionship for 'sponsorship'. It might be me, but I'm not sure that would be my first priority during a divorce!

If you go down the online divorce route, it's crucial to understand that, as with high street solicitors, not all online sites offer the same quality of help. Before you sign up, find out exactly what you will get for your money. You can always ask for feedback from people who've used their service by posting a question on a divorce forum.

Other sources of information online

There is a growing number of both non-commercial and commercial information services that have an online presence. At the time of writing, all of the sites below are active.

- A good place to start is the advice site Advicenow (www.advicenow. org.uk). It has a useful 'divorce survival toolkit' which you can download from www.advicenow.org.uk/divorce.
- Not to be confused with Advicenow's website, www.adviceguide.org.uk is provided by Citizens Advice. If you click on the left hand side of the panel (marked 'Your Family') and then click on 'family', you'll come to a section covering the ending of a marriage. Alternatively you can follow this link: www.adviceguide.org.uk/index/ family_parent/family/ending_a_marriage.htm#divorce
- www.resolution.org.uk is the organisation which many family lawyers in England and Wales have signed up to. If you want to get some basic information on the divorce process, its factsheets are a good starting point. You can download them at: www.resolution.org.uk/factsheets.
- Another site that you might find useful is Wikivorce (www.wikivorce.com), which is an online community for people going through divorce. It has a forum, a guide to divorce and a divorce calculator, which lets you work out what you might be entitled to or have to pay towards the financial settlement. Wikivorce members can also post their own articles which may be useful to others. Overall the site is very user-friendly.

Information for parents

This book is designed to focus on the financial implications of splitting up, rather than giving detailed advice and guidance on the impact of divorce on children. However, if you are a parent you may want to do some of your own research around the subject. Organisations you could try include: National Society for Children and Family Contact (www.nscfc.com), which aims to help couples who are splitting up maintain contact with their children; Gingerbread (www.gingerbread.org.uk) and One Parent Families (www.oneparentfamilies.org.uk). The government website www.direct.gov.uk is also quite user-friendly and has a page covering the breakdown of a marriage. Finally, Parentlineplus (www.parentlineplus. org.uk), although not aimed specifically at divorcing or separating parents, has some useful advice on parenting issues.

Using a lawyer

First things first. Not all lawyers are equal. Secondly, don't pick a lawyer from the *Yellow Pages* or by doing a trawl of the Internet. It's a cliché to say that personal recommendation is the best way to find a solicitor, but it's generally true. However, if you do not have family or friends who have been through a divorce, or they don't live in your area, you may have to try other routes.

Whilst it's true that you shouldn't use your lawyer for emotional support (not least because it could get expensive), it is important that you instruct someone you feel comfortable with. Your solicitor will – in all probability – see you at your very worst. Don't go with one who intimidates you or who doesn't listen to what you want.

- Talk to the solicitor to get an idea of how they communicate. It's the best way to get a feeling for how they operate. Some offer an initial advice session free of charge, but not all will. At the least they should be prepared to have a 15 or 20-minute chat with you free of charge. If they won't do that, don't bother with them.
- Don't allow yourself to be talked into signing up with a particular firm. If they apply pressure before you're a client, you can guarantee they'll be worse when they know you're paying for their time.

You instruct the solicitor. That means you have control over the type of service they provide. You can stipulate whether you want to receive an email every time you send one, or that you just want an update when something has happened that you should know about.

Types of legal help

■ Family law solicitor

■ Mediator

■ Collaborative lawyer

Family law solicitor

This is the traditional 'divorce lawyer'. Divorce lawyers used to have a reputation for being very confrontational and sometimes making an already difficult situation far worse. While that's changing – as with any profession – some solicitors are better at what they do than others and some are more expensive than others.

What a family law solicitor should do is explain what the process involves, give you an idea about the range of outcomes in terms of the financial settlement, fill in the forms for you, keep you up to date with how the case is proceeding and be available to give you advice and information as necessary. They cannot be on call 24 hours a day, but they should contact you within a reasonable time limit.

If possible, choose a lawyer who is a member of Resolution (www.resolution.org.uk) or its Scottish equivalent, the Scottish Family Law Association (www.fla-scotland.co.uk). Resolution was set up to promote a constructive, non-confrontational approach to divorce and it consists of around 5,000 family lawyers and legal staff, who have to abide by a strict code of conduct. It also campaigns on improving family law. One of the benefits of using a Resolution member is that you will be given information about all the options that are available to you, which go much further than simply using a traditional lawyer.

Mediator

What mediation is not designed to do is to stop couples who want to divorce from splitting up. Instead it will concentrate on helping the couple agree *how* they divorce through face-to-face meetings. While the mediator can provide legal information, he or she won't give you tailored legal advice. The idea is that you and your spouse can get the facts out in the open so that the mediator can try to help you discuss the financial arrangements (or whatever you need to talk about) to move the discussion towards an agreement.

Because mediators cannot give you specific legal advice, it's often a good idea to see one alongside your lawyer, rather than before the divorce process begins or as an afterthought. If you manage to reach an agreement through mediation and without the use of a lawyer, it will have to be converted into a legally binding document by a solicitor.

Many family lawyers also work as collaborative lawyers (see p. 60) and are trained mediators. If you use one who is comfortable with all the different approaches, you don't have to decide at the outset which will be best for you. However, once a solicitor has given you legal advice, they will not be able to mediate for you because of the potential conflict of interest. They would have to refer you to another mediator if you decide to take that approach.

Who does mediation work for?

The key to getting mediation to work is the quality and abilities of the mediator, rather than the dynamics of the couple who are divorcing. I've spoken to divorcing couples who have had a good experience with mediation and others who have not. A good mediator shouldn't let one person set the agenda and dominate the session, but mediation won't work unless both parties want to try it as a way of sorting out issues such as access to children or finance. As long as you can be fairly certain that you won't end up agreeing to something because you're too scared not to, mediation can work. However, it's not appropriate if there's been domestic violence or a history of intimidation in the relationship.

Sometimes two mediators will be used rather than one and some believe this is a much better approach. It means one can keep a record of what's said, while the other is able to focus on the session itself. In this situation, one mediator would normally be a lawyer; the other might have a counselling background.

Mediation is much cheaper than going to court and can be less expensive than divorcing using traditional family law. However, it may not be any cheaper than the most straightforward divorce. What's harder to put a price on is the fact that disagreements and acrimony are often dealt with more efficiently through mediation.

Finding a mediator

There are several organisations that represent mediators. The Family Mediators' Association is a very good starting point (www.thefma.co.uk). Its website has some helpful information about the mediation process. Other organisations to try are the UK College of Family Mediators (www.ukcfm.co.uk) and National Family Mediation (www.nfm.org.uk).

Collaborative lawyer

A relatively new approach which still relies on lawyers, but where negotiations are carried out in the open, is called 'collaborative law'. Some have described it as a halfway house between mediation and traditional legal advice. With collaborative law, each party has their own solicitor, but the negotiations are carried out face-to-face. Typically you and your ex would each appoint a collaborative family lawyer and have your initial telephone conversation and meeting separately, but all future discussions would have a round-table format with your spouse and both of your lawyers. It means that at all times everyone knows exactly what's being said.

The fact that everything is talked through in the open means it's far less likely that the divorce will end up going to court. There is also a further check to limit the chances of that happening – namely the lawyers who are involved in the round-table discussions sign an agreement saying if the process breaks down, they won't go to court. Instead you and your spouse would have to instruct new solicitors.

One of the advantages of collaborative law is that couples feel they have more of a say in the financial settlement; it's not just something that's imposed on them. You can find a collaborative family lawyer in England and Wales through

Resolution's site; via the Family Law Association in Scotland (at www.sfla.co.uk) and at www.afriendlydivorce.co.uk, the collaborative law organisation in Northern Ireland.

Using a collaborative lawyer normally means that the divorce process takes less time and costs less money. The main disadvantage of going down this route is that it may not be easy to find a collaborative lawyer near you. If you live in a city or large town, it shouldn't be a problem, but if you don't you may struggle.

Other professional help

Counsellor

Some law firms have counsellors or therapists attached to their practice, but many do not. If friends or family members have had counselling, you could ask them for a recommendation, but otherwise the relationship counselling service Relate is an obvious – and relatively inexpensive – place to start (www.relate.org.uk). You can get advice in person, by phone or by email. It will cost around £30 for a tailored email reply and £45 for a 60-minute telephone advice session.

Divorce coach

Divorce coaching is a relatively new concept. It isn't designed to replace the role of a lawyer, but to complement the work of other divorce professionals. Divorce coaches say that they're often contacted when someone has started the process, but isn't sure what to do next. They often encourage people to step back and work out new ways to solve the problem.

Forensic accountant

I will talk about these professionals in more detail in Chapter 10. At this stage, it's worth knowing a little about what they do and when they might be used. In simple terms, if you think your husband or wife might be hiding money in bank accounts, investments or through their business, you need someone to be able to demonstrate that. That's where specialists such as forensic accountants come in. It's their job to find hidden assets or to assess the true value of a business when parties are in dispute.

Cutting the costs of divorce

The cheapest way to get divorced is to do it all yourself. But that doesn't necessarily mean it's the best option for everyone. A combination of research on the Internet, legal help and mediation should keep the costs down. If you decide to get divorced without legal help, there will still be some costs to pay. As a minimum you should expect to pay around £350 in court costs. However, it may still be worthwhile having a one-off meeting with a solicitor to make sure you don't do anything which will prejudice you later on.

Lawyer's fees can add up very quickly. If you're instructing a partner in a law firm, you will probably pay at least £150 an hour, while a London-based firm will cost much more. Be aware that lawyers charge for their time in six-minute blocks, so if your lawyer sends you an email acknowledging one you've sent to them, that could costs you several pounds. Likewise, a short phone call may be charged at £15 (if the hourly rate is £150).

How to save money on your lawyer's fees

- Be prepared! The more information you have before you go and see the solicitor, the fuller the picture they will have of your situation. As a minimum you should try to get hold of bills and financial papers relating to you and your spouse's financial situation before your first meeting.
- If possible, make a list of your income, assets (such as property and pension), liabilities (including loans and credit card debts) and outgoings.
- Write down the questions you would like answered.

- Make notes when you are at the meeting, or bring a friend or relative who can do that for you.
- Be clear about how frequently you want your solicitor to contact you and don't use him or her as an emotional prop. The more emails they send and the more telephone calls they make, the higher your bill.

A COLLABORATIVE APPROACH

'Collaborative law seemed like a good option. I liked the fact that we'd have more say in how things worked out – and that it would be quicker and cheaper. However, we've just had our first joint meeting and now I'm not sure it will work. My husband doesn't want to discuss the pension because he says he's sorted it out. I thought the whole point of collaborative law was to go there with no pre-conceived ideas. I'll have to wait and see what happens at the next meeting.'

4 Child Support

If your divorce is amicable, you don't have to use the Child Support Agency to work out child maintenance. But if you cannot agree how much child support should be paid, then in general terms, you can only avoid using the CSA if you are wealthy and are making a claim for child support via the courts along with other financial claims. This chapter will focus on the CSA and explain some of the problems parents experience and how you *may* be able to overcome them, but it will also include information about the other options for arranging child support.

Sorting out child maintenance via the CSA can be one of the most difficult issues many divorcing parents face. On the surface it might look straightforward; one parent is supposed to pay the other a proportion of their wages, based on how many children they have and how the children divide their time. That's the theory. The reality is very different.

Many people complain that the system is unfair and that the CSA is completely unaccountable. Others aren't happy because of the lengthy backlog the CSA is dealing with or because it's made mistakes in their case. You may both believe that you have your child's or children's interests at heart, but still have very different views about how much it will cost and who should pay. For example:

- The parent who is responsible for the majority of the care may receive a lot less financial help towards the cost of the children than he or she did when the couple were married.
- Minimum recommendations for child maintenance are quite low.
- The parent who is paying maintenance and who is living away from the family home will have extra expenses associated with their new home.

They may also have the children living with them some of the time (either one or two nights a week, or more infrequently).

■ If a parent doesn't want to pay maintenance, it's quite easy for them to disappear and not keep up the financial commitment.

Who does the CSA deal with?

The CSA does not deal with all families who are going through a divorce. There are rules about situations where it can get involved. These include cases where:

■ the child is the parent's natural child or has been adopted (or is the result of IVF);

■ the child is aged under 16 or in full-time secondary education (so the CSA does not deal with children at university);

■ the child lives in the UK and the non-resident parent is either based in the UK, working overseas for a UK-based company or working overseas on government service;

■ the non-resident parent lives in a separate household to the child;

■ there is a court order in place which has been running for over 12 months. The court can make orders by consent, but after the first year the CSA can step in anyway.

Those are the rules at their most basic. If you want more information, you can look at the CSA's website (www.csa.gov.uk). In Scotland, a child aged between 12 and 19 and in full-time education (up to Higher Standard) can also apply directly to the CSA for a maintenance assessment.

When you *don't* need to use the CSA

If you and your ex can agree on child support, you may be able to make a private arrangement, without the CSA. You can either sort out how much child support will be paid between you or get a mediator or solicitor involved in drawing up an agreement. If you and your ex decide between yourselves amicably, the agreement is not legally enforceable. You may feel that you can rely on your ex to make the payments or *not* go to the CSA, but if he or she stops paying or goes to the CSA anyway, there's nothing you can do about it.

You can agree between you to make it legally enforceable by drawing up a 'consent order', which is something your solicitor can do. In limited circumstances (such as to get help with school fees), you could go to court to get a court order for child support (without involving the CSA). However, it's worth knowing that if a court order for child support has been running for more than a year, either parent can go back to the CSA to get it set aside. This is known as the '12-month rule'.

When the CSA will *always* get involved

If the parent with whom the child spends the majority of their time is on income support or income-related jobseeker's allowance, the CSA will step in – even if *neither* parent wants it to. In this case, she (or he) would not receive the full amount of child maintenance, but a maximum of £10 a week on top of their benefits (known as the child maintenance premium).

If you are receiving income support or income-based jobseeker's allowance and you don't want the CSA to contact your ex because you think it would put you or your children at risk, you can opt out. Talk to your Jobcentre Plus adviser about why you want to take this step. If they accept your reasons (in the jargon, it's called having 'good cause'), you will continue to receive your benefits as normal. If they don't, you won't receive the child maintenance premium and your benefits could be reduced by up to 25 per cent. If you feel you are not being treated fairly by the CSA or Jobcentre Plus, I'd suggest you contact your local Citizens Advice or welfare rights office.

How is child support calculated?

The first stage of working out how much child support may be paid by one parent is to decide who the parent with care (PWC) is. In many cases it will be obvious, as one parent (often, but by no means exclusively, the mother) will have the children living with them most of the time. But some parents want to share childcare as equally as they can and that's where difficulties can arise.

There are six stages to calculating child support using the CSA percentage-based formula.

1   Decide who the parent with care is. If you and your ex want to share childcare equally, the CSA will still allocate the label of parent with care to one of you. On the date of your application, the CSA will look at the 12 months preceding, which will usually have an odd number of days (unless it's a leap year). This means that – however equally you think you share childcare – one parent will have looked after the child/children more than the other, even if it's only for one night. Whoever that is, is deemed to be the parent with care.

2   Work out how much the non-resident parent's income is after tax and National Insurance.

3   Deduct pension contributions. If your resulting annual income is more than £104,000 (in 2008-09), the excess won't be taken into account by the CSA. In that case, the parent with care can apply to the courts for extra maintenance (called a 'top up' order).

4   The non-resident parent (NRP) should then deduct a percentage of their income for any children they may be supporting in their new household (i.e. child support that is being paid by the non-resident parent or his/her partner for the step child or new child). The CSA's formula states it should

be 15 per cent of your net income for one child, 20 per cent for two children and 25 per cent for three or more children.

5   You then apply the same percentages (15 per cent for the first child/20 per cent for two/25 per cent for three or more) to give a basic level of payment to the parent with care.

6   The amount of support is then adjusted according to the number of nights a week the child/children stay with the non-resident parent. If it's less than one night a week, there is no adjustment; if it's one night a week, child support is adjusted by one seventh; if it's two nights a week it's two sevenths etc. If the children split their time 50/50, there's a reduction of 50 per cent plus half the child benefit.

If your child is at boarding school, the CSA looks at how childcare was split before and after the school terms; likewise if they have spent time in hospital. If the split still works out 50:50, the CSA would deem the parent who receives child benefit to be the parent with care.

Family lawyers say that the wild card in all these complex calculations is that CSA staff don't always know the rules and – if they do – they don't always apply them. The other big problem is that few parents keep accurate information about how much time their children spend with them.

Some parents who try to share childcare find this is a real minefield. If the children split their time equally between the mother and father, it may be that one year the mother is the 'parent with care' and the next year it's the father (depending on who the children spend Christmas with). It forces parents to stick to rigid arrangements which may not be in the best interests of their children simply to ensure they don't fall foul of strict CSA thresholds.

What counts as income?

For the non-resident parent, income means earnings from a job (including bonuses) as well as payments from an occupational, stakeholder or personal pension and money received from tax credits. It doesn't include payments such as rental income, income from share dividends or interest from bank or building society accounts.

If the non-resident parent is self-employed, the rules about what counts as income are complicated. Many self-employed people operate as sole traders, but some do so through a limited company and in that case they may pay themselves a modest salary and top up their earnings with dividend payments (as a tax saving measure). However, dividend payments are not normally classed as income. If you want your husband or wife's dividend payments to be taken into the equation, you have to go back to the CSA and apply for a 'variation', when the CSA will look at matters again and usually bring the additional income into the reckoning.

The bottom line is that if you are claiming child support from your spouse and he or she is employed, with money they earn being taxed at source, you have a fighting chance of getting an accurate assessment of how much they should pay. However, if they're self-employed or run their own company, it's much more complex. They may have an accountant who manages to reduce their income for tax purposes, which may make them look less well off than they really are. CSA rules say it's down to you to get the evidence to show otherwise.

The CSA does not treat all non-resident parents the same regardless of how much they earn. If you're on a low income – below £200 a week after tax and National Insurance (around £10,000 a year at 2008–09 rates) – you will not pay the full rate.

But the CSA has got it wrong . . .

Many parents (both those who are the primary carers and those who provide financial support) complain about the amount of money they receive or have to pay, based on CSA calculations. Unfortunately, just because *you* think the CSA has got it wrong doesn't mean you will be able to get it put 'right'. In broad terms, you can only pay less if:

- the CSA has misinterpreted the facts or applied the law incorrectly;
- there are specific circumstances which mean you shouldn't have to pay the amount the CSA is stating (called a 'variation');
- your situation has changed which would affect the child support payments;
- the CSA made a mistake or a series of them when it dealt with your case and you are out of pocket as a result.

Applying for a variation

If you're receiving child support and think the assessment is wrong, it's crucial that you apply for a variation within a month of the date of assessment, so that any extra child support is backdated to the 'effective date' (the date at which you think the non-resident parent should start paying maintenance from).

Miss that one-month deadline and it's only backdated to the time of your assessment. And once 13 months have elapsed, the appeals service can't deal with your claim at all. You may feel overwhelmed by the things you have to do but, bearing in mind some of the backlogs the CSA has been struggling with, even a few days could make a massive difference to the maintenance you receive. So it's worth prioritising applying for a variation. The non-resident parent or parent with care can ask the CSA to take certain other factors into account when asking for a variation. These aren't just limited to cases where the non-resident parent may be under-declaring their income.

How child support payments may be increased

Suppose the non-resident parent runs his or her own business and seems to be living a lifestyle well beyond their means. How would you go about demonstrating that they had under-declared their income? The answer is that you would have to provide evidence for the CSA tribunal to assess, which may be easier said than done. Unless you've got expertise in knowing what to look for, you may find it very hard to convince the CSA of your suspicions.

Once the case came to tribunal, the CSA would be pretty searching. If it thought there were discrepancies between the non-resident parent's declared income and lifestyle, it would then try to come up with a figure that it calculated would be required to support that lifestyle. However, the CSA tribunal would not investigate your spouse's finances if he or she was paying for this lifestyle out of capital, or if their new partner was paying and they had no obvious control over how their partner's money was spent.

> If the non-resident parent has assets that are *not* linked to his or her business (such as savings, investments or a second property) which are worth more than £65,000, then the CSA will assume that a level of income pitched at 8 per cent a year is generated by those assets. It doesn't matter what the assets are or whether they actually produce any income or not. The rules are quite complex and it's worth bearing in mind that if you apply for a variation on the basis of 'non-linked' assets, your assessment would be further delayed while the case works its way through the tribunal system.

If the non-resident parent has other income that wasn't taken into account when the CSA worked out its calculations, he or she may be asked to pay more. Being able to get the CSA to vary maintenance payments does not mean that you will end up receiving what you think you need to pay for your children, or that you will end up paying what you think is fair.

How child support payments may be reduced

You or your spouse may think the CSA has set the levels of child support too high, but there are only limited circumstances in which payments may be reduced. These include cases where:

- the non-resident parent faces substantial travel costs (normally of over £15 a week) keeping in touch with his or her child or children;
- he or she has to meet expenses incurred in relation to the long-term illness or disability of another child in their household;
- he or she is paying boarding school fees for the child, in which case the boarding element of the fees (not the teaching element), assumed to be 30 per cent, may be taken off the income before running the calculation;
- he or she is paying the mortgage of the house where the parent with care is living;
- he or she has to pay debts which were run up for the joint benefit of both parents or for the benefit of the child. However, not all money you or your spouse might count as debt can be included. For example, fines, credit card debt, legal costs, business-related debt, money that is owed to friends or family and bank overdrafts do not count.

Even if you or your spouse has extra costs to pay that meet the criteria in the list above, it's worth knowing that these costs are not taken off the amount of child

> support that the CSA calculates should be paid, but
> are used to reduce the non-resident parent's income.
> So if you pay £100 on debt payments every month,
> your child support payments aren't cut by £100 a
> month, but by £15 a month if you were supporting
> one child, £20 a month if you were supporting two
> children and £25 if you were supporting three or
> more children.

Non-co-operation by the non-resident parent

If your spouse is the non-resident parent (NRP) and he or
she doesn't want to pay, the CSA has several sanctions.
Some are more effective than others.

- If the NRP provides misleading information or doesn't give the
  information in the first place, he or she can be fined by up to £1,000
  for each failure.
- The CSA can apply a default maintenance assessment of £30, £40 or
  £50 per week (depending on how many children you have).
- CSA inspectors can try to get information that's not been provided by
  the NRP. If necessary, they can use their 'right of entry' powers (but in
  reality these are rarely, if ever, used).
- The CSA can take maintenance that's owed directly from the NRP's
  salary through a Deductions from Earnings Order (or DEO). However

the scheme cannot be used against a sole trader or someone who is willing to move jobs to avoid payment.

■ The CSA can obtain a Liability Order from a magistrates court. The Liability Order gives the CSA rights to apply for further court orders which will enable it to freeze money in bank accounts, put a charge on property or even to take way the driving licence of the NRP.

■ Ultimately the CSA can ask for non-payers of child maintenance to be sent to prison.

The CSA has been described as having rather a 'trigger happy' approach to deducting maintenance directly from the non-resident parent's salary through DEOs. There have been cases where, two years after an application to the CSA has been made, the CSA sends out its assessment of how much should be paid, closely followed by a DEO.

Stumbling blocks and traps

While parents who end up paying child support may resent the amount of money that the CSA calculates they should pay – especially if they've also had to give up the majority of the capital in the family home – some parents who approach the CSA for help with maintenance complain that their spouse is able to run rings around the organisation. The truth lies somewhere in between. If you believe you are entitled to more child support than is being paid, it may be because your spouse is able to manipulate the system by disguising how much he or she earns, by paying more into their pension or by taking on extra responsibilities. You can complain to the CSA, but it won't be able to turn over every stone to find out exactly what the true financial picture is.

Although it does have powers and penalties that it can apply when necessary, you may feel that your ex is 'getting away with it' and that the CSA isn't up to the job. The law in this area is technical and complex and it's quite possible that the person you speak to on the phone doesn't have the expertise that's needed or doesn't know enough about the history of your case.

If, however, you're paying child support, you may feel you're being taken for every penny you have. Or you may be bewildered by the powers the CSA has at its disposal. At the time of writing, the CSA was known to be pursuing a number of non-resident parents for thousands (and sometimes tens of thousands) of pounds in back payments – money the CSA said they owed, despite their claims that it had never contacted them with an assessment in the first place. Even if the NRP had paid support throughout that time, unless he or she had proof, the CSA expected the back payments to be made in full.

The criticism the CSA has received over the years is one reason why it's being replaced by another organisation called C-MEC (the Child Maintenance and Enforcement Commission; see p. 84). But until this is up and running, you will have to deal with the CSA and some believe that the CSA's replacement will be no better and may be even worse.

Where to get help

If you're getting nowhere dealing with CSA staff, try divorce or parents' websites and forums for advice and information. You can guarantee someone else will have had a similar experience to your own, although you are unlikely to get advice from a qualified expert. Otherwise you could get in touch with the child support advice group NACSA (www.nacsa.co.uk), which offers free general advice and email support. It aims to help both parents with care and non-resident parents, but says it receives most of its enquiries for help from non-resident parents who feel they have nowhere else to turn. If you want one-to-one advice by telephone, it costs £40 a year to join. NACSA is also a campaigning organisation which believes the CSA (and its replacement C-MEC) is fundamentally flawed because it only targets 'easy wins'; namely non-resident parents who are likely to pay up.

Advantages of using the courts

Some solicitors advise clients to sidestep the CSA by combining an application for child support with one for maintenance for themselves. This may not be possible (if you're not entitled to spousal maintenance) and is likely to be expensive, as with all divorce cases. But if you are entitled to maintenance, it's worth considering, particularly where your ex has a complex financial situation or you have to pursue a court case because your financial claim includes pensions or other assets. However, the court is prohibited from awarding you spousal maintenance to replace payments that should be arranged through the CSA.

While the CSA can only look at child maintenance, the courts can order:

- that child maintenance is paid where the CSA cannot get involved, such as when children are at university, when they are abroad or when the non-resident parent is living abroad;
- that child maintenance is paid for the cost of school fees;
- that child maintenance is paid for the costs associated with having a disabled child;

- that 'top up' child maintenance is paid where the non-resident parent earns more than £104,000 a year (after tax and NI have been deducted), which is the CSA's upper income limit;

- that maintenance is paid by one spouse to the other (as long as they have divorced and the spouse who is applying for maintenance has not remarried);

- that, in some cases, maintenance is paid to a husband or wife who have separated but not divorced;

- that lump sum payments are made;

- that a pension is either split, offset against the value of other assets or earmarked (where some of its value is ring-fenced for one spouse's retirement);

- that maintenance payments are made or assets are divided where one parent has died.

Court powers if your ex won't pay

If you have a court order, the good news is that the law is on your side in that there are sanctions you can use. The problem is that it costs money to use them. The ultimate deterrent is that you can have your ex arrested if he or she won't make maintenance payments, but you'll have to balance the actions you *can* take with the financial and emotional costs. If you cannot track down your ex in the first place, it can be hard to take things further. And if your ex is genuinely unable to pay because he or she has higher expenses, there isn't much you can do, as pressing ahead with the case is likely to result in him or her returning to court to reduce the award.

Child maintenance post-CSA

At the time of writing, the government has announced plans to replace the CSA with C-MEC, the Child Maintenance and Enforcement Commission. There isn't much detail about how the CSA's replacement may work and whether it will be an improvement on the current system, but already there are a fair number of sceptics who are convinced that its introduction won't result in fundamental change.

What we know at this stage is that C-MEC is supposed to:

- encourage parents to make their own child maintenance agreements;
- simplify and streamline how child maintenance is calculated, so that money gets to parents (and therefore children) more quickly;
- get tougher with parents who don't pay maintenance.

ZERO INFLATION

'Friends told us that CSA was a nightmare, so we avoided it like the plague. We agreed between us how much maintenance I would pay. At the time I was earning quite good money and we decided on 20 per cent of my income for our two children, but I'm earning less now so it's probably more like 30 per cent. It's capped so it stops when my youngest reaches 18, which is in 11 years' time, so I think that's fair.'

5 The family home

SELLING UP

'My husband is still living in our house, although I've recently moved out with the children. It's just gone on the market, but I'm a bit worried that he's going to try to make things difficult when we sell. Some people came to see it last weekend and my husband said he couldn't show them round, so I had to drive back to make sure someone was there. The couple didn't have anywhere to sell and were really keen, but my husband has said he won't move out until he's bought somewhere. It means we may lose the sale.'

The home you've shared during your married life will probably be the most valuable asset you own and it's also likely to be the one that has most emotional significance. If you've invested a lot of time and effort in making your house a home, you may find the process of selling up and moving out particularly hard. And if your ex ends up owning the house, but you pay some or all of the mortgage, you may feel resentful if you're forced to pay for a home that you can no longer live in.

On the other hand, your worries might be much more practical. Where will you live? If you have children and they will live with you for the majority of the time after your divorce, will you be able to stay in the home that your children love and which may be near their friends and a school they're settled in? Will you be able to get a mortgage? Will you be able to afford the payments? What happens to your home is likely to depend on whether or not you have children, how much money you have and what other assets you own between you.

Many couples find it particularly hard to keep their emotions out of the equation when dealing with the family home, but you will get a much better result if you can manage to do so. If you can work out what will happen in a reasonably amicable way, so much the better. If you can't, it will come down to what the courts decide. Bear in mind that if you end up in front of a judge, you might still emerge no better off than if you had worked it out between you.

What to do

- Don't worry about sorting everything out relating to the house in one go. Break down what you need to do into manageable chunks.
- Separate out your list of worries or concerns into emotional issues, issues concerning the children and those relating to the house.
- Work out what you'd like in an ideal world (in terms of where you would prefer to live and how many bedrooms etc. you want the property to have), but be prepared to compromise.
- Keep in touch with your mortgage lender and any other company that has lent you money secured against the value of your home.

Next steps

Whether you're going to sell up and each buy a smaller property, or one is going to buy the other out, or part or all of the property will be transferred from one to the other, there are several steps you will have to take. They may include:

- valuing the property
- changing the ownership of the property
- unravelling your existing mortgage
- assessing the mortgage options

Valuing the property

Whatever your reasons for selling, you will need to get the property valued. Have a look at house prices in the area to give you a rough idea of how much similar properties are being marketed for. Websites such as Rightmove (www.rightmove.co.uk), Primemove (www.primemove.com) and Propertyfinder (www.propertyfinder.com) are good places to start. Then ask for a valuation from three different estate agents.

If you're getting a valuation because you want to sell, rather than because one of you plans to buy the other out, it's worth putting a bit of effort into the presentation. Unless the housing market is roaring away, when house buyers are just grateful to be able to afford a home of their own, they will be put off by grubby walls, smelly pets and bodged DIY jobs. Ask a friend round for a 'viewing' and be prepared to listen to their advice. If you don't have the time or expertise to sort it out on your own, ask a local handyman (or woman). Try the government-supported scheme Trustmark (www.trustmark.org.uk) or a commercial site such as www.problemsolved.co.uk to find a reliable tradesperson.

> If you're selling up and each buying a new property, it can make the process more complicated as both you and your ex may be in a chain. In order to ensure the sale goes through, you may have to be flexible about

completion dates etc. If one person has moved out and is keen for a sale while the other doesn't want the home to be sold in the first place, it can create a real tension. In extreme cases, one party can try to sabotage the sale (overflowing ashtrays throughout the house, a sofa in the front garden and no heating in winter have all proved very effective, according to estate agents I've spoken to!). Unless you've both agreed amicably what should happen, tell the estate agent that you are getting divorced when you sign the firm up. They deal with sales from divorcing couples all the time and can sometimes anticipate problems before they arise.

Changing the ownership of the property

It is possible for you to change the way you own property (if you live in England, Wales and Northern Ireland) from joint tenants to tenants in common. The advantage of doing this is that if you die before your divorce comes through, your half of the property won't pass to your ex. It's a fairly straightforward process: one of the owners needs to serve a 'notice of severance' on the other. If the property is registered, you should contact the Land Registry so that a 'restriction' can be added to the title deeds. However, it's a double-edged sword in that if you sever the joint tenancy and the co-owner falls under a bus, you will no longer automatically inherit their half of the property and will have made an expensive mistake!

In Scotland, the situation is more complicated. Most jointly owned properties are owned in a way that's similar to tenants in common, which means they don't have a 'survivorship clause'. If the title has a 'survivorship destination', it's similar to owning as joint tenants. To change the title you need to 'evacuate' the survivorship destination. As well as sounding unattractive, it's a complex process which you need expert legal help to carry out.

Unravelling your existing mortgage

Whatever happens to the former matrimonial home, the chances are that you will have to unravel the mortgage. How straightforward this is will depend on a number of circumstances, such as what type of loan it is and how much money you have. If you have signed up to a special deal (such as a fixed rate or tracker mortgage), there may be an early repayment penalty (although mortgage lenders get a bit skittish about the word 'penalty' so call it an early repayment charge or ERC).

If the family home is being sold and you are each buying another property, you may be able to avoid the ERC by 'porting' the mortgage (i.e. taking it with you). Obviously only one of you can do that. If it's a joint mortgage, the other person needs to sign a letter waiving their right to port the loan. There have been cases where the divorce is so acrimonious that neither will agree to the other moving the mortgage, which means the lender imposes the penalty. Try to avoid this scenario because the only winner will be the mortgage lender.

If you bought your property at the top of the market, especially if you have a high loan-to-value mortgage (such as 90 per cent or more) you may be in negative equity – where your mortgage is worth more than the property – when you come to sell. That's especially true if you added the cost of arrangement fees or a higher lending charge (which used to be called 'mortgage indemnity guarantee') to the costs of your loan. At the time of writing this book, house prices were predicted to fall by anything from 5 per cent to 20 per cent and more.

Some types of mortgage are easier to unravel than others. Your mortgage will be:

- repayment
- interest-only

Repayment

With a repayment mortgage you should ask your lender for a redemption statement, which says how much you need to repay, including any penalties. As well as early repayment charges you may have to pay an exit fee, which can cost up to £300. The benefit of a repayment mortgage (apart from its simplicity) is that you pay off some of the capital every year, which reduces the chances of negative equity.

Interest-only

If you have an interest-only mortgage, your monthly payments only repay the interest, not the original amount you borrowed. You should ask your lender for a redemption statement in the first instance. The complicated part of unravelling interest-only mortgages comes when you try to deal with any investments (such as endowments or ISAs) that you may have in place to pay them off.

Endowment

Endowment-backed mortgages are structured so that – in theory at least – the endowment policy pays off the amount you originally borrowed at the end of the mortgage term. Your endowment provider should send you annual statements of how much your policy is worth, but these don't tell you how much you might get if you cashed it in.

To find that out, you need to ask the endowment provider for a 'surrender value'. If you're thinking of paying off your mortgage rather than one of you taking it over, you will have to work out how you can extract the maximum value from your endowment.

You can:

- cash your endowment in
- leave it invested but not pay any more money into it
- try to sell it on the second-hand market

Cashing it in

This is the simplest option, but it's the one that could produce the least money. If you cash it in, the company you have the endowment with will pay you what it is worth, minus any penalties for surrendering it early. These may include a charge called a 'market value adjustment' or 'market value reduction', which are normally imposed when the stock market has fallen sharply or is very volatile, but under the terms of the contract, companies can do so pretty much whenever they choose.

Leaving the policy invested

If you can't afford to pay the monthly premiums, you could leave it invested or 'paid up'. You don't pay any more money; instead the endowment company deducts charges and premiums to pay for life insurance (that is built into all endowments), from the fund.

Selling it on the second-hand market

With some types of endowment policy there is a third option; selling it on the second-hand (otherwise known as 'traded endowment') market. However, not all endowments can be sold this way. To sell it your policy it has to be:

- a with-profits policy
- five years old or older
- worth £1,500 or more if you were to cash it in

There are three types of endowment policy; with-profits, unit-linked and unitised with-profits. Ignore the off-putting jargon. All you need to focus on is whether or not your policy is with-profits. The information will be on your annual statement, but if you're in any doubt call the endowment provider.

If you type 'sell your endowment' into a search engine, you'll see the names of dozens of different traded endowment companies. My advice is to go straight to the

Association of Policy Market Makers (www.apmm.org), which represents half-a-dozen traded endowment specialists. You can download an application form to get a free no-obligation valuation of your endowment from all six members of APMM and see whether you'd get more than if you were to cash it in. The quote is normally valid for a week or ten days (depending on the company) and if you decide to go ahead, the sale should take six to eight weeks to be completed.

When you cash in your endowment or sell it, you also give up the life insurance and any critical illness cover that goes with it. If you bought the endowment when you were much younger – and especially if you have suffered a bout of ill health since then – you may find it is much more costly to replace the cover. If you need a new quote, try the specialist broker Lifesearch (www.lifesearch.co.uk).

Individual Savings Account (ISA)

If you're using an ISA (or a series of them) to pay off your mortgage, you should write to your ISA provider for an up-to-date valuation. If you want to cash it in, you may get back less than you expect – or even less than you've paid into it – if the stock market has taken a tumble. If the ISA is in your spouse's name, you can't transfer it to your own because of the tax benefits.

Assessing the mortgage options

Redeeming your mortgage should be relatively straightforward, but it can be more complicated if one of you wants to take over the existing loan. In the first instance you need to contact your mortgage lender, who may ask for a fee to cover administration costs. You will also need to ask a solicitor to carry out the legal work. If you don't have one, your divorce lawyer should suggest someone.

Problems and how to overcome them

Lenders will only allow a mortgage to be transferred from joint names to a sole name if they're confident that the borrower can afford the mortgage payments. If they won't allow the transfer, it may mean the person whose name stays on the mortgage can't get a new loan in their own right. And even if they agree, you or your spouse may not have a large enough income for a mortgage of your own. You may experience one of the following problems:

- your lender won't allow the mortgage to be transferred to sole name;

- your existing mortgage means a second loan is unaffordable;
- you have no capital for a deposit.

Lender won't allow the mortgage to be transferred to sole name

This problem often arises when one spouse, for example the husband, is the sole or main earner, especially if the wife has little income in her own right and relies on child maintenance and/or spousal maintenance. Mortgage lenders won't normally count maintenance as income, so in that case the husband's name may have to remain on the mortgage. One solution would be to remortgage with a more sympathetic lender – in particular, one that will count maintenance in the same way as ordinary income when working out how much to lend.

The alternative is to find a 'guarantor' (such as a parent or other relative), who promises to make the mortgage payments if you cannot afford them. It's not a decision they should take lightly, as they will be making a legal commitment to the mortgage lender and it would affect how much they could borrow if they wanted to buy a second property or move house.

Don't assume all banks and building societies take the same attitude; they don't. Although many mortgage lenders will not treat maintenance as income, some do. A good independent mortgage broker will be able to tell you which are worth approaching and which are not. If you need a broker, I'd suggest you try Charcol (www.charcol.co.uk), which does not charge a fee for arranging a mortgage. Another is Savills Private Finance (www.spf.co.uk), which deals with mortgages above £100,000 and typically charges 0.4 per cent of the value of the loan.

Maintenance with court order

If your maintenance is being paid with a court order, you will have a better chance of getting a mortgage than if it's not. If you want to borrow a relatively low loan-to-value mortgage, say, below 75 per cent of the property's value, a court order will give you access to a bigger choice of lenders. For loans higher than 75 per cent, your choice of lenders will be severely restricted without a court order.

Even with a court order, the mortgage lender will want to know how long the maintenance payments are supposed to last for. If your children are in their late teens, you may only receive maintenance for another couple of years, which could cause a problem if your mortgage term is longer.

Maintenance without court order

There are lots of advantages to avoiding the courts and sorting everything out as amicably as possible, but there are disadvantages as well. At the time of writing, there were only two mortgage lenders who were prepared to consider maintenance payments without a court order as income (and as one is a subsidiary of the other, it only really counts as one company).

Yorkshire Building Society and its subsidiary, Accord, will both accept maintenance payments with a letter from a solicitor stating what has been agreed. Maintenance, unlike most other income, is tax-free to the recipient, so £1,000 a month maintenance is worth more than a salary of £1,000 a month. Both Yorkshire Building Society and Accord will take that into account when calculating how much they will lend.

Yorkshire Building Society will also lend up to 95 per cent of the property's value, although before the credit crunch it would lend 100 per cent. In case you're wondering why it's getting such a big mention, I don't have any affiliation or financial relationship with the company. I just think it's worth highlighting a lender that's doing something different. Lots of divorcing couples try to sort out maintenance payments without a court order, but few mortgage lenders seem prepared to acknowledge this.

Some lenders who don't take into account maintenance can be persuaded to look at individual cases on their merits if they have a good relationship with your mortgage broker. It may come down to a decision by one person at the bank or building society (the underwriter looking at the case) and if they trust the mortgage broker because they've dealt with them over a number of years, they may look at the case much more sympathetically. You may think it's unfair that a mortgage broker could get a mortgage accepted that an individual could not, but that's the reality of today's mortgage market. If you go to a good broker, they could make a real difference to your situation.

Your existing mortgage means a second loan is unaffordable

You may be as keen for your spouse to come off the mortgage deeds as he or she is, but if you don't have enough income to pay the mortgage on your own (and you can't find a guarantor), it may not be possible. This will affect your ex as well as you because it will almost certainly mean that he or she will be able to borrow less.

Whether or not your ex actually makes a payment towards the mortgage on the home you live in, he or she will still be treated as doing so by the lender if their name is on the loan.

Increasingly, mortgage lenders take affordability rather than income multiples into account when working out how much to lend, which means they look at how much you earn and how much you already have to pay by way of commitments such as maintenance, loans, credit cards and so on. Most lenders will be comfortable with 35–40 per cent of your gross income going on commitments such as these. However, if you pay more in mortgage or maintenance payments, or if you're still on your ex's mortgage, the amount a lender will be prepared to lend you will be reduced. Again, not all companies have the same approach and some will let you borrow more than others.

Make sure you don't fall foul of capital gains tax (CGT) if you're transferring property. Transfers between husband and wife are exempt from CGT while you're still married, so if you transfer your home from your name to your ex's, there will be no CGT to pay if it happens before the divorce is finalised. However, if your name has to remain on your ex's mortgage while you're separated but before your divorce comes through, there may be a CGT liability. If you have separated and own your own home and own or have a share in another, you will fall into the CGT net.

To make sure you don't incur a potential liability, you can divide ownership of your properties between you and your ex on a 'tenants in common' basis and ask your solicitor to draw up a declaration of trust, which states what portion of the property each partner owns. For CGT purposes, each partner could take a 1 per cent interest in the other's property. If either of you sells your property, you will be liable for CGT on 1 per cent of the price. So even if property prices rise by £200,000 over a period of years, you would only be liable for CGT on £2,000, which would fall within your CGT allowance (£9,600 in 2008-09). Any profit below your CGT allowance means there is no tax to pay.

You have no capital for a deposit

If you don't have any money for a deposit, the answer may be to try to find a 100 per cent mortgage. However, at the time of writing no lender was offering them. This is likely to be a temporary state, but lenders will also be more cautious for some time after the credit crunch than they were before. Even if you were able to get one, they come with a bit of a health warning because the interest rate is often considerably higher than on a 90 per cent mortgage and there's also a danger of negative equity. Negative equity is only a problem if you need to sell while prices are lower, but as life can be unpredictable (as anyone reading this book will be able to testify), it's a risk you should be aware of. Get advice from a good independent broker.

Normally when property is sold or given away, stamp duty is payable on the proceeds, but this doesn't apply if property is transferred between husband and wife as part of a court order for a financial settlement in divorce. However, if one of you agrees to buy the other out, stamp duty should be paid. Take advice from your lawyer.

Credit problems and how to overcome them

One problem that many divorcing couples experience is that they get behind with bills or just can't make ends meet. The bad news is that this could have an impact on your chances of getting a mortgage (or one at a competitive rate). If you're going through a divorce, you may feel that you have more important things to worry about than the odd missed payment, but don't bury your head in the sand when it comes to money.

It may not be *your* money management that causes a problem; sometimes an ex-husband or wife who is moving out of the family home will not feel under such an obligation to pay the mortgage once they no longer live there. Others may not pay out of spite. But if your name is on the mortgage, it will affect your credit record if you do not make the payments. If you think your credit status has already been affected, or you want to find out what the situation is, get a copy of your credit file. There are more details about how to do this on p. 145 in Chapter 8.

If your credit rating has suffered, your broker should be able to point you in the direction of lenders that take a sympathetic approach. Some banks and building societies will get very nervous about taking on borrowers who have had any hint of credit problems – even if they are minor – while other high street names may be more flexible.

Sub-prime (or adverse credit) mortgage

Before the credit crunch of 2007, Britain had a growing 'sub-prime' sector, catering for people with bad credit records, but it shrank in rapidly towards the end the year. At the time of writing, an increasing number of sub-prime lenders wouldn't lend more than 75 per cent of a property's value and their interest rates have risen sharply. What this means is that even if you can get a sub-prime mortgage, you may not be able to afford the payments.

My advice would be to steer well clear of specialist sub-prime brokers, no matter how bad your credit record is. You *may* be able to get a loan from a mainstream lender if your credit problems are minor and happened at least two years ago (in some cases, even a 12-month gap will be enough). But if you can't, going to a sub-prime broker is not the answer. Many specialist sub-prime brokers charge fees of between three and five per cent of the value of the loan; the interest rates can be significantly higher than elsewhere and some sub-prime lenders have a reputation for being swift to take repossession action if you fall behind with your payments.

Build up your credit history

If you can't get a mortgage (or can't get one that doesn't want to charge you an arm and a leg for the privilege), try building up your credit history. By paying your rent/mortgage, credit card and utility bills on time you will demonstrate to lenders that you are a reasonable credit risk. If you've only got behind with your credit card and other bills, a lender may reconsider you after six months' clean payment history, but if you've missed mortgage payments, you would probably have to wait for a year.

SPLITTING THE COSTS OF ONE HOME INTO TWO

'I've got a mortgage in place for £200,000 – thanks to my father, who's agreed to act as a guarantor. It means I can buy somewhere big enough for me and the three children. As a couple, we had a mortgage of £335,000 but we have very little equity in the house and we've got some credit card debts to pay when we sell it. My husband says that if I can spend £200,000, he wants to be able to do the same. I just feel that he's not being realistic.'

6 Spousal support

FINANCIAL SUPPORT

'My husband agreed to pay maintenance for our children and for me while the children are still at school. I've only worked part-time since we had the children whereas he's been in a very well-paid job. It actually took about 18 months to agree because he didn't want to co-operate with filling in all the forms, although it didn't get to the stage of a court order. What the maintenance means is that I've been able to afford to buy somewhere of my own.'

Maintenance for the spouse is not an issue for the majority of couples who get divorced. However, although ongoing maintenance is only paid in a minority of cases (and is very rare in Scotland), its negotiation can be fraught with difficulties. Maybe it should not be entirely surprising: there's no straightforward formula for working out who should get what and some couples are poles apart in their ideas about what's fair.

If you're seeking maintenance, you may be tempted to make your ex pay as a way of punishing them for how they've behaved during the divorce or marriage. Conversely, you may resent the fact that you've worked hard to reach your current standard of living, while your ex is seemingly entitled to a percentage of your income without lifting a finger. Try (no matter how hard it may be) not to let emotions get the better of you. It's true that you may be able to change the terms of the deal by negotiating (or fighting) via your lawyers, but it's also true that you could spend *a lot* of money, time and energy in doing so.

> If you are the party asking for maintenance, your solicitor should try to keep you focused on what is really at stake: namely, can you support yourself after your divorce and what standard of living is realistic, bearing in mind that you will both be affected financially by the break-up?

What is maintenance?

Maintenance is designed to provide an income for a spouse who is unable to support themselves, or in the case of very high earners, to compensate one party for having given up a career to stay at home and look after the family. It can be paid on a short-term basis to give the person who's either given up work to look after children, or who has a much lower earning capacity some time to get back into the employment market or to retrain for a new career.

It can also be paid on a long-term basis where there's been a long marriage and one person cannot realistically support themselves to a high enough standard or where they cannot work for other reasons. Although the courts will take a variety of factors into account (such as the length of the marriage and your health), they have a lot of discretion when it comes to how much maintenance should be paid and for how long.

Because only a minority of divorces ever get to court, the level of maintenance often comes down to what the lawyers are able to negotiate on your behalf – albeit from a starting point of what the courts will take into account. In very basic terms, the older you are when you get divorced, the longer you've been married and the higher your standard of living when you were married, the more likely you are to receive maintenance.

The courts will take the following factors into account.

■ The length of the marriage. In general terms, the longer the marriage, the stronger the claim for maintenance.

- Your health. If one of you is ill or unable to work, that could affect the amount and length of maintenance.
- You and your spouse's age. Generally, the younger you are, the more likely it is that you will be able to work and to earn more from your employment or business over time.
- Past standard of living. The standard of living you enjoyed when you were married will probably have an impact on the amount of maintenance you receive, but not necessarily on the length of time you receive it for.
- Job sacrifices during marriage. Maintenance may increase if one spouse turned down job opportunities so that the other could take the work that he or she wanted.
- Education and employment skills. Your educational qualifications, employment experience and the length of time you have been out of the job market may all affect the amount of maintenance.
- Parental time. The courts may decide that spousal maintenance should be increased if child care responsibilities mean you are limited in the types of job you can do.

What are the options for the courts?

If you apply for maintenance, how it's paid may well depend on where in the country you get divorced. Ongoing maintenance is rarely paid in Scotland, as courts aim for a clean-break settlement. In England and Wales, whether maintenance is paid is often down to the area you live in. For example, in London, where the cost of housing is so high, it is very difficult to get a clean-break order when there are children involved: even if the courts only make an order for a nominal amount of spousal maintenance (which could be as low as £1 a year), they would prefer to do that rather than make a clean-break order. In Northern Ireland, clean-break settlements are preferred, but maintenance can be paid.

The court has a duty to consider a clean-break settlement in every case and if it can achieve this it will. But many couples simply don't have enough capital to support this type of settlement, especially if one partner hasn't worked for the majority of the marriage. Unless the income payments can be capitalised (which means that you would receive your ongoing maintenance as an upfront lump sum), ongoing payments would be the only option.

Where maintenance will be paid, the starting point is what the spouse in question needs. Beyond need, the court would look at entitlement to share one person's income and/or compensation for having given up their career. However, in the vast majority of cases, need is the only factor that comes into the equation. The court can make several orders for maintenance:

- periodical payments
- secured periodical payments
- lump sum order

Periodical payments

These may be weekly or monthly payments. If you receive unsecured periodical payments, they would not continue after the death of your ex.

Secured periodical payments

These types of orders are rarely made. Unlike periodical payments orders, they do not end when the ex spouse who is paying maintenance dies. Instead, the payments are secured against assets (usually held in a bank account to which the payer has no access).

Payments made for a specified length of time are called 'term orders'. There are two types: extendable term orders and non-extendable term orders. The assumption in both cases is that payments would stop at the end of the term, but if you have an extendable term order and have been unable to find work and support yourself, you can go back to court and ask for them to continue. However, you must apply before the end of the original term. Meanwhile a 'joint lives' order will continue until either person dies or the one receiving maintenance remarries.

Lump sum order

One spouse may be ordered to pay a lump sum to the other. As its name implies, this arrangement is normally one single payment but in some circumstances it can take the form of a series of instalments.

Negotiating maintenance

The starting point for negotiations is to demonstrate how much you need, but it's not an exact science. For example, if you didn't work during part or all of the marriage (perhaps because you were bringing up children), the courts wouldn't expect you to work immediately after the divorce, but if you were relatively young, the assumption would be that you would be able to return to the job market at some point. You wouldn't be forced to take a particular job by the courts (or even to work at all), but they would be free to assume you were capable of earning a certain level of income with your experience and skills and *could* reduce the amount of maintenance you would be awarded.

When working out your budget, you would have to take into account any income from work you already do and other sources of income as well as benefits you may already receive, or may be entitled to (such as child benefit and tax credits). There's more information about applying for tax credits on p. 150 in Chapter 8. However, it can be difficult to get anything approaching an accurate prediction of your future entitlement to benefits.

Although benefits you receive may affect the amount of maintenance you are entitled to, maintenance is not taken into account when working out whether you are entitled to benefits such as working tax credit.

Reviewing maintenance

Once maintenance has been decided, its level is not set in stone. If you're receiving regular payments and start living with a new partner, your ex may try to get the payments reduced. However, this is not automatic as maintenance continues at the level set by the court until the court makes a new order. If you're the spouse paying maintenance through a consent order, you should apply to the court for a variation of the order if you and your ex cannot agree to vary it.

You need to apply to the court that dealt with the original order. Some orders may include a nominal maintenance payment for 12 months in case the relationship fails; which means the ex receiving maintenance could go back to the courts within that time and ask for a higher level of maintenance. However, if you're the payer, you do not have to accept the nominal maintenance provision. Your solicitor will be able to advise you on the best option.

Trying to prove that your ex lives with a new partner can be tricky. You could start by checking the electoral roll, but your ex or the new partner may continue to live at another address for 'official' purposes. In some cases, it comes down to having a private investigator sitting outside the house to show how many nights someone's ex and their new partner spend together.

Interim maintenance orders

If you're applying for maintenance, your solicitor will probably recommend that you make an application for an interim maintenance order (or 'maintenance pending suit', to give it its correct legal term) if you cannot agree it between you. This is basically a maintenance payment while details of the divorce are finalised and it's typically made where one partner is the main or sole income earner.

There have been discussions about extending the courts' powers in relation to interim orders for a number of years, with no result. The fact that the courts have such limited powers means there are circumstances where they cannot actually make an order; for example if one spouse has a large amount of capital and no income and the other has very little money of their own.

DEMONSTRATING NEED

'I was asking for maintenance from my husband because I had three young children. The youngest was only two when we started divorce proceedings. I had to write a paper on how much I thought I could earn in the coming years. I'd sold my business when we got married and hadn't worked since we'd had our first child. My husband's solicitors said I should be able to start another business, but my earning capacity is much lower because I have to build my day around the children.'

7 Pensions

DIVORCING THE PENSION

'I never made a claim on my ex-husband's pension, even though he's in the Forces and has access to a really good pension scheme. I was paying my own legal bills and at the time I just couldn't afford to let things drag on any longer. People have said that I shouldn't have given up my claim on his pension. I don't have one of my own and I am a bit worried about what I'll do as I'm in my fifties, but at the time, I felt as if I didn't really have a choice.'

As a nation, we're not saving enough for our retirement. For many of us, the age at which we should start putting money aside for our retirement is when we're either paying off debts run up when we were students, or struggling to buy our first home. Figures from the Association of British Insurers estimate that collectively, adults in the UK need to save around £27 billion *a year* more than we're currently saving. At first sight, that figure is so large as to be almost meaningless (although if you break it down, it actually only works out at just short of £700 for every adult in the country).

The point is that most of us don't have enough to retire on and some of those who have the least are women, especially women who have taken a career break to bring up children or who get divorced later in life after a long marriage. The rules relating to the way pensions can be treated during divorce were changed in 2000 so that any company or private pension (and some parts of the state pension) can be split at the time of divorce. Previously, the only options were to offset the value of the pension against other assets (the pension would stay intact but the other party would take a larger share of something else – typically the family home) or to earmark part of it for the spouse to take at retirement.

Pensions jargon

One of the reasons why pensions can still get overlooked in divorce cases is that they're shrouded in technical and off-putting jargon. It's easy for most of us to understand the concept of selling up or taking some value out of the family home and it may not be difficult to work out why an estate agent has valued it at a particular price. But with pensions, it's not nearly so straightforward.

Many of us who have a pension aren't entirely clear about what we've signed up to. So here's a quick guide to the different pension options. It will help you understand the terms that your pension company or solicitor may use and it will also give you an insight into why pensions sharing is not straightforward.

Final salary pension (otherwise known as 'defined benefit' or DB pension)

Here you earn a percentage of your salary at retirement (normally 1/60th or 1/80th) for every year you're a member of the scheme. The amount you have to contribute varies according to how generous the scheme is.

Money purchase pension (otherwise known as 'defined contribution' or DC pension)

Instead of being promised an income at retirement based on your salary, the money you pay into your pension goes into a large fund (or several different funds). The amount you receive at retirement depends on how much you and your employer have paid in and how well the investments in the fund have performed over that period.

Group personal pension (or GPP)

This works in a similar way to a money purchase scheme, in that the amount you get at retirement depends on how well the fund has performed and how much has been paid into it. The main difference is that it's treated in the same way as a personal pension, which means you can take it with you when you move to a new job. Employers don't have to contribute to GPP schemes if they don't want to.

Stakeholder pension

Stakeholder pensions were introduced in 2001 as a low-cost and flexible option for those with no pension. They can be bought directly from a pensions provider or arranged through your employer. As with money purchase schemes, the amount in the fund depends on how well the investments have performed. If your stakeholder scheme was arranged through your employer, they may or may not make contributions to it (they don't have to by law). If it's a pension you've taken out directly with the pensions company, the only money going into it will be the payment you make.

For the purposes of simplicity, I've described the main types of pension scheme, but as pensions have developed over many years there's a mind-boggling array of schemes that I've not mentioned here. If you want to know more, I suggest you look on the Pensions Advisory Service website (www.pensionsadvisoryservice.org.uk), which is an independent and free advice and information service.

At the time of writing, there is one significant planned change to pensions that is creating a lot of debate. The government is committed to introducing what are called 'personal accounts' in 2012. A personal account is a new style of pension which is designed to encourage more employees to save for their retirement. Currently, a number of company pensions have relatively few members. The plan is that employers pay 3% of a worker's salary, employees pay 4% and a further 1% comes from tax relief.

Valuing the pension

If you or your spouse has a money purchase, GPP or stakeholder pension, you may underestimate just how valuable it is. Let me explain why. The true value of a pension is down to the mysteries of 'compound interest' or 'compound returns'. It means that a fund that's not worth much in the early years (say, when you've got 20 or more years before retirement), could grow significantly by the time you actually reach retirement age. The easiest way to explain it is in relation to savings. If you put £1,000 in the bank earning six per cent interest, you will have £1,060 at the end of the first year. At the end of the second year, you will earn six per cent interest on £1,060, so will have £1,123.60 and so on.

Although investments don't normally rise by a predictable percentage every year (because the assets they invest in, such as shares, property and bonds can fall as well as rise), the same principle applies. If your fund goes up in value one year, the following year any growth applies to the original value of the fund plus the increase in value from that year. So, a pension fund that is worth £50,000 today could be worth around £137,000 in 15 years' time (assuming it grew by seven per cent a year). Walking away from half of £50,000 might not seem like such a big deal (to some people at least), but walking away from half of £137,000 could be another matter.

Some pensions are more difficult than others to place a value on and to try and unravel, which is why the types of pension(s) that you and your ex have are relevant. Although many divorcing couples may underestimate the value of a money purchase pension or GPP, as far as the experts are concerned, it can be more difficult and time-consuming to work out how much a final salary pension scheme is worth.

Pensions options

Even though the pensions sharing rules were introduced some years ago, it took a while for some solicitors to take them on board. But most are more aware of the importance of pensions. If yours doesn't seem prepared to prioritise the pension, consider approaching an independent financial adviser (IFA) for advice, unless the pension fund in question is very small. There are three ways that the pension could be divided:

1 offsetting
2 earmarking
3 sharing

Pensions offsetting

This option has been available to divorce lawyers for many years and is the most common way of taking the value of the pension into account. However, it has its limitations. Firstly, if the pension is by far the biggest asset, what's left may not be valuable enough to be offset by it. Secondly, whoever is left without the pension has to make their own retirement arrangements. Depending on their age and available income, they could find it very difficult to make up for lost time. And while pensions have restrictions on how old you have to be before you can cash them in, they are much more flexible than property (such as the family home) when it comes to retirement. Many people plan to rely on their property to provide them with a pension in retirement, but unless they are considering downsizing significantly, it's not practical.

Pensions earmarking

A law change in the mid-1990s allowed part of one partner's pension to be ring-fenced or 'earmarked' during divorce, so that the other could receive it at retirement. However, the earmarking option has never really taken off and there are several reasons for this. The person who benefits from pensions earmarking (normally, but not always, the ex-wife) has to wait until their ex retires before they can receive any payment, so if the ex-husband is younger or simply decides to carry on working beyond retirement age, she will be left without a pension income. And if she remarries, she loses her entitlement to the earmarked pension altogether. If her ex-husband dies, she would also lose her pension income as most schemes wouldn't class an ex-spouse as a dependant (although you could get round this problem by taking out life insurance).

Pensions sharing

This was originally supposed to be called 'pensions splitting', but by the time it became law, its name had changed to something that sounded altogether more amicable. It's essentially about dividing the pension that one partner has built up so that it can provide retirement income for two. On the surface, it may sound relatively straightforward, but it can be quite a complex and time-consuming process. Don't be surprised if your divorce lawyer starts calling in pensions experts if there's a large pension fund that needs to be taken into account. A mistake in valuing it could have long-term consequences for both parties.

> Be warned! Negotiations around the pension could take up a lot of time and effort. If you're the party making a claim, you may be tempted just to settle as quickly as you can, but I'd advise against it. Most people don't have enough money for their own retirement and you could really struggle in later life if you don't take the pension into account.

The pensions sharing process

Both you and your ex will have had to give details about your pensions (either through a form E if you're in England and Wales or through disclosure of assets if you're in Scotland or Northern Ireland). However, these only ask for a straightforward overview of someone's assets and can't cope with the complexities of pensions. In England and Wales, pensions form P asks for more information, but not all family lawyers use it. Even then, it may be hard to get all the potentially relevant information required to build up an accurate picture of the situation.

Once a value for the pension has been arrived at, there may be different options available to the person receiving the pension. In most cases, they will be given a lump sum to use to start their own pension, but sometimes they will be able to join their ex's pension scheme and have a pension paid at retirement, based on the benefits of that scheme.

Cash equivalent transfer value

The cash equivalent transfer value, or CETV, is the starting point for working out the value of a pension. In broad terms, it's an interpretation of how much the pension is worth at that moment if it were to be converted into a cash sum. It's relatively straightforward to work out the CETV if the pension is a defined contribution pension or a personal or stakeholder scheme, as they are all valued in a broadly similar way. With occupational money purchase pensions, those who run the scheme, called the trustees, have to provide the information, whereas with personal or stakeholder plans, it's down to the pension company that you have your pension with.

With defined benefit (or final salary) pension schemes, it's not so straightforward to get an accurate 'snapshot' valuation and pension scheme trustees can be slow at getting the information together. There are other reasons why the CETV can be something of a minefield. Many family lawyers consider that the CETV is the universally accepted measure of working out how much a pension is worth, but that's not always the case.

Many pensions experts say it's worth getting the CETV checked by an actuary to make sure it's been calculated correctly if the fund is significant in size. Don't consider it if the pension fund is small or medium sized, but it may be worth involving a pensions specialist if the pension is reckoned to be worth £100,000 or more (but bear in mind that the initial £100,000 valuation may not be accurate!). You will have to evaluate the potential gains of getting accurate information against the costs of doing so.

Catches and complexities

There are all kinds of ways in which what looks like a plausible figure for the CETV of a pension may not be accurate. And even if it is, the proposed division of the pension may not necessarily be fair.

Pension underfunding

Because final salary pension schemes guarantee to give
the pension scheme member a specified level of pension
at retirement, their value at a particular time is less
relevant. For example, if investment returns are mediocre (or
worse) one year, your employer might be forced to pay more
money into the scheme to top it up. The pension valuation
taken in the 'bad' year would reflect a low valuation, but the
scheme member would still receive what they were expecting
at retirement. If a scheme is underfunded, it would have to
let the ex-spouse join it until it was in a position to provide
a normal (i.e. not reduced) CETV.

Preferential retirement terms

Some final salary pension schemes, such as those for the
fire brigade, police force and armed forces, allow a scheme
member to take early retirement without penalty. This will
not be reflected in the CETV, which will be based on
benefits at normal retirement date.

Guaranteed annuity rates

With money purchase schemes, you build up a pension
fund which you have to convert into an annuity so you can
receive a monthly income. (There are some exceptions to
this rule, but as describing them would take several pages,

I'm ignoring them. Visit www.moneymadeclear.fsa.gov.uk for information.) Some money purchase schemes may include a 'guaranteed annuity' rate, which means that the scheme member could get a much better income from the same fund than someone without the guarantee, but this would not be reflected in the CETV.

Market value reduction

Another problem that can complicate the valuation of money purchase or personal pension schemes is a market value reduction. It only applies to pensions where some or all of the fund has been invested in a with-profits fund. With-profits funds invest in a mixture of shares, cash, bonds and often property as well. From time to time, providers of with-profits funds may impose a market value reduction (MVR) on policyholders who want to cash in their investments early. If the CETV includes an MVR penalty, it would be lower than if the fund was allowed to remain invested until the scheme member retires.

Tax-free cash

Normally at retirement you can take 25 per cent of the fund you've built up as tax-free cash. However, with some schemes – for example, those for company directors – you can take a higher level of tax-free cash; sometimes significantly higher. If you were a company director with a pension fund worth £150,000, which you could take entirely as tax-free cash, you would receive £75,000 tax free (assuming a 50 : 50 split on divorce), whereas your spouse could take only 25 per cent of £75,000, i.e. £18,750 as tax-free cash. The rest would have to be taken as an annual income, on which he or she would pay tax.

Equitable value

Suppose you have a divorcing couple where one partner (let's say the husband) has a pension with a CETV of £500,000. If it was a final salary pension scheme that was being divided, the husband might have been in line to receive £30,000 a year at retirement before the pension was shared. If you wanted to split that 50 : 50, you might assume it would be divided so each partner received a fund of £250,000. But because women live longer than men and therefore receive a lower annual income from a pension fund, a 50 : 50 split would mean the ex-husband would have a higher annual income (assuming that his ex-wife was of a similar age and health).

State pension

Although an occupational or private pension will often be far more important than the state pension in terms of value, you are also entitled to a share of your spouse's state second pension (the replacement for SERPS), as part of any pensions sharing order. But you may be able to increase your own state pension entitlement after divorce as well.

The amount of state pension you get at retirement is based on the number of years you have paid National Insurance (NI) contributions for (or had credits for them, if you have been looking after your children or caring for a relative). In order to get a full state pension, you have to have paid 39 years' NI if you're a woman and 44 years' if you're a man, although if you're due to retire after 6 April 2010, the number of years you have to pay NI in order to get a full state pension is reduced to 30 for both men and women. Once you're divorced, you can claim a state pension based on your ex-husband or wife's NI contributions record (for the years while you were married), if it's better than your own.

Under the current system, you can only start receiving a pension based on your spouse's NI record once they have claimed their own, but for those retiring after 6 April 2010, this restriction is lifted. Your ex still has to have reached pension age, but if he or she has chosen to delay taking their state pension (called 'deferring' in the jargon), you can still claim yours. For free, impartial and expert advice on this matter I would suggest you contact the Pensions

Advisory Service (www.pensionsadvisoryservice.org.uk or 0845 601 2923).

SHARING THE PENSION

'We'd been married for 25 years by the time we got divorced. My husband was in a well-paid job with a good pension while I worked part-time and looked after our two children. When the lawyers found out how much my husband's pension was worth, they advised me to hire a senior barrister – a QC – rather than a junior barrister. I'm still not sure what he did apart from add to my legal costs. I did get half my husband's pension, though, and that has made a huge difference to me.'

Mastering your finances and minimising debts

FROZEN OUT

'When things were at their worst during the divorce, I went to our joint bank account and found he'd frozen it. The bank was really unhelpful. They told me that while my husband was able to freeze the joint account on his own, it would take *both* our signatures to unfreeze it. I spoke to my personnel department at work and got my salary paid into a different bank account. It caused some problems but because I was working, I had money of my own. If I hadn't had that, I'd have been penniless and it would have been a nightmare.'

The chances are that you and your ex will have mixed together your money – to a greater or lesser extent – while you've been married. What you have to do when you get divorced is separate it. If you're on reasonable terms, this should be relatively straightforward; you just need to prepare yourself for a lot of form-filling. If you're not, you'll have to try to find the right balance between protecting your own financial position and not making an acrimonious situation worse.

The basic rule is that while your name is still on an account, you're liable for any debts on it and if you have a joint loan, you're each responsible for the entire amount, not just your 'half'. If you've moved out of the family home, you may also have your name on bills that you think you should no longer pay. I've already covered the mortgage in detail in Chapter 5, so this chapter will explain what you need to do in relation to other accounts and will give you some time and money-saving tips as well. The finances you will have to sort out may include:

- bank accounts
- credit and store cards
- council tax
- utilities
- insurance
- bank loans
- hire purchase agreements

Bank accounts

Your first step is to contact the bank or building society where you have joint accounts and ask for the account to be closed or for your ex's name to be removed. However, not all banks take the same approach and some make the process easier than others. As a general rule, you will both have to sign a letter if you want the account to be closed or converted to a sole name, although a number of banks will let one person freeze the account.

Some banks will offer other options such as taking away the overdraft facility or asking for two signatures rather than one before any transactions are authorised. If yours won't let you do this, or if joint signatures are not a realistic option, you will have to close the account.

If your account is overdrawn, you won't be able to close it until the overdraft has been paid off. Try to reach an agreement about how it will be repaid, but keep an eye on the account. If your ex is being very difficult, you may have to weigh up the benefit of paying off the overdraft (if you can afford it) so you can stop him or her from getting you both further into debt, against the cost of doing so.

Credit and store cards

If you and your ex each have a credit or store card from the same account, you might assume it's a joint account, but there's no such thing as a joint credit card in the UK.

The account has to be in the name of one person only (the principal cardholder), while the secondary cardholder is not legally responsible for any debt arising from money they spend on it.

If you're the principal cardholder, you should contact your credit card company and tell them what's happened. Normally you'll be asked to destroy the second card if you want to continue with the account, but if you can't get hold of it, you will have to ask the card company to block the whole account (they can't block one card only). You'll then have to draw up a new agreement in your name alone. Don't forget to cancel any payment agreements that your spouse may have set up (but tell him or her before you do it).

Tell your ex what you're planning to do before you act. If you genuinely believe they may go on a revenge spending spree, at least inform them the moment you've cancelled their card. Don't let them find out when they're at the till unless you're happy for bad feelings to escalate.

Council tax

If one of you moves out and the other remains in the former matrimonial home, the one remaining is responsible for paying council tax. Don't forget to apply to the council for a single occupancy discount of 25 per cent if you will be the only adult living at the address (some other adults, such as full-time students are exempt).

Utility suppliers

Most gas and electricity suppliers let you cancel your contract online if you're moving home (and you don't have to be billed online to do it). If one of you is taking over a supply that was in the other's name, it's a little more complicated. If you want to come off the account, contact the supplier as quickly as possible because the gas or electricity company will not backdate any usage to someone else's name, only to the point at which they've been notified of the change.

If one person wants to take over what was a joint account, it's normally a straightforward process once the meter reading has been received. However, if there are any arrears on the closed account they will be pursued in the usual way, which could ultimately involve debt collectors. Contact the consumer watchdog Energywatch, at www.energywatch. org.uk, (or its replacement from 2009, the National Consumer Council at www.ncc.org.uk) if you're worried about the way your gas or electricity company is dealing with your case.

If you and your ex have to close accounts from your former matrimonial home and would prefer minimal contact with each other, you might be interested in a website called Moveme (www.moveme.com). Moveme lets each of you close accounts that are held in your own name and will inform the other partner by email when it's been done. If you're moving to a new house, you probably won't want your ex to know what accounts you are opening, so the website will only let you see information relating to the house you shared, not to each other's new properties.

Insurance

If you have insurance cover (such as a household or contents policy) and you want to remove one of your names, you will normally have to confirm this in writing. Some insurers may take instructions by telephone, if they can verify who you are. The value of the contents in your home may reduce once your ex has moved out, so tell the company as it could result in lower premiums. If you're looking for insurance for your new home, shop around. Different insurance companies target different types of customer and yours may not be the best value for you. There are details about different price comparison sites on p. 144.

Changing details on your car insurance should be straightforward if you're simply removing your ex's name from your own policy, but if you've been a named driver on his or her policy, you will have to take out a new one in your own name. Shop around at price comparison sites and insurance brokers. The British Insurance Brokers' Association has a list of brokers on its website (www.biba. org.uk). You can search by area or for one that specialises in a specific type of policy.

Loans

You cannot simply convert a joint loan into one in a sole name. You should either pay it off and set up a new one if you need to, or try to come to some agreement as to who will make the payments. There may be an early repayment penalty on the original loan, while you may be charged a higher rate of interest for the new loan if your credit record has been damaged in the meantime or if the bank has tightened up its lending criteria.

Debt advisers tell me that sometimes a repayment plan is drawn up by a divorcing couple – which they have every intention of sticking to – but which ultimately fails. This can cause real problems and will damage the credit records of both you. If either of you gets behind with repayments on a joint loan and the bank does not have up-to-date address details for you both, it will contact the person whose address it has and, if your ex has moved out, that will be you.

It doesn't matter who has benefited from the loan, all the loan company is interested in is whose name is on it. If one of you took out a loan (perhaps because your credit rating was better than your spouse's) so that the other could buy a car, for example, the person whose name is on the agreement must take steps to make sure the monthly payments are made, or pay off the loan completely.

Hire purchase (HP) agreements

If you bought a car on hire purchase and you cannot keep up the repayments, you should contact the company concerned. Hire purchase agreements are different to ordinary credit in that you don't own the goods until the last payment has been made. However, once you've paid more than a third of the total debt (including a deposit and any part-exchange), the company must have a county court (or sheriff court in Scotland) order before it can repossess the goods.

You can end an HP agreement by writing to the finance company and requesting an early settlement figure, provided the agreement is regulated by the Consumer

Credit Act. This figure is likely to include a penalty charge of one month's interest. If you return the car in a condition beyond 'fair wear and tear', then you may be liable for an additional charge. Legally you are entitled to return the car to the finance company with no further obligations once 50 per cent of the total amount payable is paid. If you're served with a notice of default, you can go to the courts to request a 'time order', so that the payments are reduced for a specified period of time.

If you buy your car through hire purchase, you're the 'registered keeper' until the last payment has been made, while the owner is the car finance company. This can cause a problem if the car was bought on HP by one spouse as a gift to the other. If the spouse who took out the agreement doesn't keep up repayments, the car could be repossessed. If it gets to the stage where the finance company wants to repossess the car and it doesn't have up-to-date address details for the keeper, it may register the vehicle as stolen.

Finding help if you're in debt

Many people find it difficult to admit they need help and you may feel unable to face up to the realities of your finances while you're going through a divorce. But I'd recommend that you contact a debt adviser if you're having problems making payments on your loans – and the earlier you ask for advice, the more they can do to help. Some people worry about what the debt adviser may think about the state of their finances, but I guarantee they'll have seen it all before and no-one will judge the decisions you've made.

Debt advice services worth contacting include the Consumer Credit Counselling Service (CCCS). It offers advice over the telephone or, if you prefer, you can be counselled anonymously online. You can contact them at www.cccs.co.uk, or on 0800 138 1111. Alternatively, try National Debtline (www.nationaldebtline.co.uk). Its website has a useful range of leaflets to download, as well as sample letters to send to companies you owe money to. You can also contact them by telephone free on 0808 808 4000. I'd also suggest you try Citizens Advice (www.citizensadvice.org.uk), which has bureaux in many towns and cities. All give debt help and some have specialist money advisers.

Because debt advice services like these have a wealth of experience in dealing with financial companies, they will be able to help you if you feel as if you're getting nowhere or that the bank or credit company is ignoring you. Many companies will charge you a fee to sort out your debts and they may be perfectly competent, but why would you pay someone for debt help when a lack of money has caused the problem in the first place?

Be aware that (at time of writing) if you type 'National Debtline' into Google, you may get a sponsored link that takes you to companies that are not the debt advice charity.

Getting a better deal with price comparison sites

Price comparison sites are designed to take the hard work out of shopping around for a better deal on anything from home insurance to electricity, credit cards to savings accounts. While they generally *do* take the strain out of comparing different deals, many are highly profitable in their own right and most are directly financed by the companies they recommend – either by getting a commission when you switch to that company or a small payment when you click through to their site.

Unfortunately, they're not normally upfront about how much they make from recommendations and some display information in a way that guides you to the companies that pay them commission. The other problem is that different sites can come up with different results that they say are the best deals.

I'd recommend that you compare the results you get from at least three sites. Some to try are: www.money supermarket.com, www.uswitch.com, www.moneynet.co. uk, www.moneyfacts.co.uk and www.switchwithwhich.co. uk. If you're shopping around for gas or electricity, always go to a site that has been accredited by a consumer watchdog. That means it has to display the tariffs of all companies, including those that don't pay it any commission. And don't forget the Financial Services Authority's own comparative tables at www.moneymade clear.fsa.gov.uk. They're put together by the financial regulator, so you can be guaranteed they are impartial.

How are you rated?

Your next step is to see what information is stored about you on your credit file. It's the only way to find out what kind of credit rating you have and whether there are any problems you need to deal with. Credit files are used by hundreds of different companies whenever they want to work out whether or not to lend you credit. Financial companies like banks and credit card providers have always taken credit information into account, but these days it's scrutinised a little more carefully.

There are three credit reference agencies: Equifax (www.equifax.co.uk or 0870 0100583), Experian (www. experian.co.uk or 0870 2416262) and Call Credit (www. callcredit.co.uk or 0870 0601414). Although a lot of the information they hold overlaps (in that most lenders supply information to at least two of the credit reference agencies), it's worth getting your file from all three if you want to be absolutely sure that you know what information is held about you. You have a statutory right to see a copy of your credit file if you pay a £2 charge. Some credit reference agencies insist you do this in writing; others will let you order it online.

Normally I'd say it's worth checking your credit reference file once a year or so, but if you're going through a divorce, you should keep a fairly close eye on it, not least because your ex's credit record may be rather shakier than your own. And unless you do something about it, their bad credit record could affect yours too.

You may be able to see your credit file for free if you sign up to a trial of one of the credit reference agencies' credit report monitoring services. The trial period normally lasts for 30 days and you have to give your credit or debit card details when you register. You must

> cancel your subscription within the 30 days or you'll
> end up paying a monthly fee (sometimes up to £9).

What's on file

Your file contains information about where you live, plus
addresses you've lived at over the past six years. It also shows
whether or not you're on the electoral roll (which gives
evidence to lenders that you are who you say you are). Any
County Court Judgements (CCJs) that are registered against
you (called Decrees in Scotland) will be listed and will
remain on file for six years. Your file will also show whether
you've been declared bankrupt (called 'sequestration'
in Scotland) or entered into an individual voluntary
arrangement (IVA) within the last six years.

The most important part is a list of all the credit
agreements you have and have had over the last six years.
Details include how much you owe, how much the original
debt was for (or what your credit limit is if it's a credit card),
the term of the loan, when the credit agreement was taken
out and whether you're up to date with your payments over
the last 12 months.

> If your credit file isn't as good as you were expecting,
> don't panic! Check the details to make sure that

what's being said about you is correct. There may be some unfamiliar names on your file. That doesn't mean it's a mistake; often store cards are supplied by third party companies so you might not recognise them. However, if there *is* a mistake on your file you can have it put right. Tell the credit reference agency what you think is wrong and they'll contact the lender on your behalf (known as 'raising a dispute'). The agency has to get back to you within 28 days and give you a progress report and in the meantime, any information that you have queried is marked as 'disputed' and the lender is not allowed to rely on it when deciding whether or not to give you credit.

If your credit file shows that you've missed or been late with payments on a credit card or loan, you can add an explanation of up to 200 words (called a 'Notice of Correction') as to how this happened. If you don't, all lenders will see is a series of numbers showing whether or not you've made payments on time. Once you've submitted it, it should sit at the top of your credit reference file, so lenders see it before they look at any other information about how you've managed money you've borrowed.

When it comes to credit information, what's important is both how serious the problem is and how recently it happened. If you missed one payment on a loan and applied for more credit within weeks, lenders would take a dim view of it. If it happened a year ago, they would be less concerned. Some lenders would be prepared to ignore one missed payment if your credit rating was otherwise impeccable (as they'd assume you'd been on holiday), but more than one and they would probably think differently.

Financially-related items

Credit reference agencies are only allowed to link your credit information to that of anyone else you have a 'financial relationship' with (i.e. a joint loan or mortgage). You can ask for the credit reference agency to take your ex's details off the credit file, but only once you've closed any joint loans or bank accounts, you no longer share the same address and you have an independent income. You do this by asking for a 'Notice of Disassociation' from the agency. Once you've asked for the changes to be made to your file, it's worth getting hold of a copy to make sure it has been updated.

State benefits

Depending on your financial situation, you may be entitled to state benefits including child tax credit and working tax credit (although there are other benefits you may be able to claim). The government website Directgov (www.direct.gov.uk) is a useful starting point.

Tax credits

Tax credits are dealt with by H M Revenue and Customs (HMRC) and you can get basic information on how they work at www.hmrc.gov.uk/taxcredits or you can ring the tax credit helpline (0845 300 3900). There are two different types of tax credit which you may be eligible for as a parent:

- child tax credit
- working tax credit

Child tax credit

The good news about child tax credits is that – according to government figures – 90 per cent of families (with either one or two parents) are able to claim some financial help. The benefit is paid to the main carer of the children and it doesn't matter whether or not that person is in work. The amount of income is calculated per household rather than per person and in basic terms, the household is eligible for child tax credits if it receives no more than £58,175 a year or £66,530 if you have a child aged under one year (for tax year 2008–09). If you are close to the threshold, you will only receive a minimum amount.

The bad news is that applying for child tax credit is not straightforward. Working out how much you may be entitled to is complicated and some of the staff who handle claims give out contradictory advice. The amount you get is set for a whole year, so if your income changes you could be entitled to less (or more) than you are receiving – and the onus is on you to tell Revenue and Customs if your financial circumstances change. I'd still advise you to apply because you may otherwise be turning down money you are entitled to and CTC can only be backdated for up to three months. Make sure you keep detailed records about your application.

Working tax credit
If you're in work but on a low income (whether you're employed or work for yourself), you may be eligible for working tax credit. How much you are entitled to will depend on how much you earn and other circumstances. The credit is made up of several different elements, including a childcare element which is worth up to 70 per cent of eligible childcare costs up to a limit of £175 a week

(£300 for two or more children). I could fill several pages with information on how much you may be entitled to and what affects the amount you get, so instead I'll refer you to www.direct.gov.uk or a website called 'entitled to' (www.entitledto.co.uk), which helps you work out which state benefits you may be eligible to claim.

UNEXPECTED DEBTS

'When we got divorced, I found out that my husband had all kinds of credit card debts and loans that I didn't know about. It was a complete shock. He'd never told me about his debts in the 33 years we were married. It was difficult because it meant that after we'd sold the house and paid off the debts, we were in negative equity. It's taken me a couple of years to recover from that financially.'

Valuing a business and finding hidden assets

PUTTING A VALUE ON A BUSINESS

'I don't think my husband had thought about the impact of divorce on his business. He'd sold it a year before we got divorced and had received half the payment upfront. He was due to get the rest a couple of years later and I think he believed that only half its value would be taken into account. My solicitors ended up employing some expert accountants to look at exactly what he'd received from the sale. I think he thought I was trying to fleece him, but what drove me was fear. Fear about my own future and that of my children.'

Dividing assets such as savings, ISAs and shares can be difficult enough, but at least it's usually fairly easy to value them. However, it may be different with a business that either you and your ex own together or one of you owns outright, particularly if it's not publicly quoted.

153

If you and your ex can sort out issues around how much the business is worth through straightforward disclosure, so much the better. If you can't agree, there's a wealth of expertise available to you, but the experts' time can be quite costly. Even though divorcing couples are obliged to enter into 'full and frank disclosure' of their assets, there's no guarantee the information is accurate. Owners have been known to value their businesses at £1,000, based on the fact that there's only £1,000 in the bank, or at zero because the firm has never been sold!

If you've never been involved in your partner's business and your break-up is acrimonious, you're more likely to be suspicious that they're playing down its true value. But suspicion alone may not get you very far. Your solicitor will want information about why you think the business may be worth more than your spouse is declaring and where you think the discrepancy may lie. You may only have a vague idea, but the more details you can provide, the more you will reduce the costs of finding out its true value.

Financial settlements have moved increasingly towards an equal division. As the business could be one of the biggest assets, splitting everything 50:50 may be impossible without dividing the business. The courts won't flinch from ordering the sale of a business, a division of shareholdings or refinancing for one party to buy out the other's interest if it's necessary.

Gathering information

It's unlikely that your ex will leave his or her company accounts lying around and there are rules about what you can and cannot do to get hold of information. But a little bit of research may help.

- If your ex runs a limited company (rather than being a self-employed sole trader), check the website of Companies House (www.companieshouse.gov.uk) to see what you can find out about the current business and whether he or she is a director of any other companies.

- Your ex's self-assessment returns for the last three years will show how much he or she earned and declared to HMRC and how that has changed.

- If the company is small enough to file abbreviated accounts, Companies House records are virtually worthless as they don't contain a profit and loss account. Instead, you'll need the full company accounts and financial statements for the last three years to establish whether the business is becoming more or less profitable.

- You'll also need supplementary information like details of directors' remuneration (including basic pay, dividends, bonuses and any benefits in kind) and abnormal or one-off income/expenditure in accounts.

- Trust deeds, shareholder agreements or other documents that show how your ex acquired his or her interest in the business and the current ownership structure (which may affect how the business is to be valued) are also useful.

- If you have details of bank loans, actual balances outstanding and security provided for the loans (including any loans or debts that you or your ex have personally guaranteed), they will add to the picture.

Until comparatively recently, a small number of divorce lawyers seemed happy to encourage their clients to try to get hold of information about their spouse's financial circumstances by questionable means. The family courts tended to take the view that this information could be used in proceedings, although if it was obtained by unlawful methods, they could impose a financial 'penalty' in the way the legal costs were split or in a reduced financial settlement. Now there are signs that the courts are assessing differently the way information is gathered. It's a grey area, but one that solicitors are becoming much more aware of. The rule of thumb is that you can 'self help' when it comes to documents, but you're not able to break into a filing cabinet or hack into a computer.

Businesses in Scottish divorces

Under the Scottish system, businesses and shareholdings in companies are only taken into account if they were set up or acquired after the marriage. This can cause a problem if your ex set up his or her business before you got married, but it did not start trading until after the wedding. However, one advantage of the Scottish divorce system is that it is easier to get hold of information if an ex is being uncooperative. If documents are not forthcoming, you can ask the court for a 'Commission and Diligence' order. To get one, you have to prepare a 'specification of documents' that lists the paperwork you believe you need to prepare your case for the financial negotiations. If the court agrees with you, it will approve the list and you can then approach any party you need to (such as accountants, banks etc.) to get the information direct. This means you can bypass your ex entirely. The party you serve the court order on has to produce the information you've requested within seven days and sign a certificate stating that it's correct.

How a business is valued

There are several ways that a company can be valued. You don't have to have a detailed knowledge of how each method works, but it's useful to understand the basics. The main methods are variations on:

- earnings basis
- assets basis
- dividend basis

Earnings basis

This is the way the majority of profitable businesses are valued. Essentially, it looks at the profit stream that a company could generate in the future and multiplies that figure to determine a value. The multiple figure is chosen by the accountant (or whoever is valuing the business) by benchmarking the firm to similar quoted and private companies. Economic and other factors are also taken into account. For example, if it's owned by both parties, could it survive if one left? Does it have more borrowing than is healthy?

Assets basis

Where profits are erratic or non-existent, the assets basis is useful. It's also employed for certain types of business, such as property investment or development, where the value of the company will be closely linked to the value of the assets it owns. Here, an accountant would look at what the company would be worth if the assets were sold in the ordinary course of business as a going concern. If the firm's future trading isn't looking viable, the valuation might be done on a liquidation basis, which would give a lower figure. It's only relevant if your ex holds more than 75 per cent of the shares in the company, as you cannot wind up a company without control of less than that percentage of the shares.

Dividend basis

If your ex has a minority shareholding in a company (i.e. below 50 per cent), you might get a more accurate idea of its worth with a valuation done on a dividend basis. For example, you might have an established family business paying a dividend of £10,000 a year, which could be worth more than the underlying assets the business owns. A minority shareholding might also not be valued highly on the open market, but may be worth more to someone who already owns a larger shareholding in the company and who wants to increase it.

It's better to use forecasts of what the business owner expects his or her company to do in the future than to look back at how it's performed in the past, especially where it's gone through a start-up or some significant event or change. However, very small companies may not prepare forecasts at all, or the projections may be unreliable and they may be influenced by the purpose they were prepared for. If your ex has produced a forecast to secure a loan from the bank or to attract a buyer, it might paint the fortunes of the business in a rather rosy glow.

Tricks of the trade

If your spouse has a business, there are a number of ways in which he or she could reduce its value for divorce purposes. Your solicitor or forensic accountant will be on the lookout for them. They include:

- Overpaying the business owner. Paying the boss an inflated salary or benefits, reducing the company profits.
- Underpaying the business owner. In the run-up to a divorce, the owner of a business may cut his or her salary significantly, saying the business can't afford it.

- Overpaying workers. A spouse may pay their girlfriend or boyfriend a salary through their business without them working for it.
- Sharp downturn in fortunes. A business may suddenly and mysteriously hit hard times once the owner knows that a divorce is looming.
- Diverting income. This may include setting up a related company that then charges the main business for its time, reducing the money that is left.
- Bringing in friends as business partners. Setting up a second company (such as a management company), but using friends to run it.
- Provisions in accounts. Undervaluing stocks and debtors, or overvaluing creditors.
- Over-funding the owner's pension scheme to reduce profits temporarily.

Often the partner who owns or has a shareholding in the business is very pessimistic about what it's worth, while the person with no involvement is equally optimistic. You may believe your spouse's business is worth a small fortune. You may even have been told it's worth that and have lived the lifestyle. But it wouldn't be the first time that a husband or wife has lived beyond their means. Just because you've led a particular lifestyle doesn't mean it was actually supported by the business.

The role of experts

If you or your solicitor thinks the valuation of the business is not accurate, you may want to call in a professional to check the figures. 'Forensic' accountants specialise in working out the true value of a business and in uncovering hidden assets. Many family lawyers use them where there is a dispute over the value of the business, and in the first instance they may ask one to have a preliminary look over the figures to see whether it's worth investigating. This could cost several hundred pounds. If you want to take things further, you will have to instruct a forensic accountant formally and costs are likely to increase to several thousand pounds.

These days it's normal for divorcing couples to instruct one professional expert between them (called a 'single joint expert'). The idea is that you and your ex don't run up huge bills trying to prove that your suspicions are correct. However, if a particular forensic accountant has been informally contacted by the solicitors acting for one party (as outlined above), they cannot be used as a single joint expert because impartiality is paramount. They're also not allowed to meet one party without the other being present, or without their explicit approval.

It's still possible for each of you to instruct your own forensic accountant (called a party expert), rather than relying on one you've jointly appointed. Often it's down to the judge whether he or she will accept each side using their own forensic accountants, but a single joint expert may be used when the business is not the main focus of the case.

> The single joint expert has an overriding duty to the court and not to either party. It wouldn't be unusual (or necessarily wrong) for one to come up with a valuation that leaves him or her with two disgruntled customers; the business owner may believe the valuation is too high while the other party may think it is too low.

Hidden assets

Some people going through divorce suspect that their ex will go to almost any lengths to avoid disclosing their true worth, in which case they may prefer to get some expert evidence to back up their suspicions. However, you should be warned that it's possible to spend thousands of pounds trying to prove that your ex has money salted away in a bank account or an offshore trust, and still not get a definitive answer.

Forensic accountants will normally give you an appraisal

of whether they think it is worth trying to track down hidden assets or whether you risk spending a lot of money for nothing. Whatever you spend on professional fees will reduce the amount available to split between you. It's also worth remembering that the courts will only act on evidence that you (or your forensic accountant) manage to produce.

Using legal powers to uncover hidden assets

If you believe your ex has money in a particular bank account and is not being forthright, you can apply for a Search Order. However, it's rarely used as you have to have evidence that they are hiding something; you cannot use it to go on a 'fishing expedition'. A Freezing Order (or injunction) is useful if you're worried that your ex is going to dispose of assets without telling you, as it covers assets held both in the UK and abroad. And if your ex has not complied with a specific order, your solicitor can issue him or her with a Penal Notice. Ultimately, he or she could be sent to prison, although that happens very rarely as you have to prove beyond reasonable doubt that they've breached the order.

Private investigators

You might think that private investigators are only used to gather evidence to prove adultery, but there are some specialist firms which also undertake hidden assets work. Some family lawyers work with private investigators, others prefer to use forensic accounts and some use both. Talk to your lawyer about who he or she uses. If you use an investigator, make sure they're a member of the ABI (not the Association of British Insurers, but the Association of British Investigators) and that they have experience of tracing assets (and not just errant partners) in divorce cases.

In Scotland, the Commission and Diligence court order I mentioned earlier can be used in hidden asset cases as well as to value a business. The advantage of this document is that you don't have to know where assets are hidden to request information. For example, you could serve it on every bank near your former marital home as well as your ex spouse's independent financial adviser and his or her accountant and lawyer. However, you can also serve it on your ex, if you think that they have information that they have not disclosed.

HIDDEN IN THE FIGURES

'I'm convinced my husband is hiding assets. He owns his own business and some of his accounts have mysteriously gone missing. I've been told they go too far back for him to be able to provide them, but I think he's stalling. I've asked for other information but he's just said no. I've pored over his business accounts, but they simply don't make any sense. I think my next step may be to use a forensic accountant. I'm aware it'll be expensive, but it's the only way I'll get some answers.'

10 Troubleshooting

ADDING UP THE COSTS

'Looking back, I wish we'd used mediation, but I think we were caught on a wave of emotion. I'm a very emotional person, whereas my ex-husband is very businesslike. He clicked into corporate mode and we just fought. In the end, his legal bill was £100,000 and mine was £70,000. I admit I sat on things, but I couldn't deal with the paperwork; I was so scared by it all. I think I allowed the solicitors to take over and ratchet up the bad feeling. Seeing my husband in court arguing over how much he'd pay for our children was very distressing.'

You probably never thought divorce would be easy, but you might not have expected it to be this hard. Some people do manage to divorce amicably, and with a range of legal options available aimed at reducing the stress rather than fanning the flames, that number should rise. However, if your spouse is determined to dig his or her heels in or if your divorce started badly and it's only getting worse, you may feel there's little you can do. Some things will undoubtedly be outside your control, but there are steps you can take to improve your situation and plenty of sources of help and advice to enable you to get there. In this chapter I'll look at different areas where you may experience problems and give you some tips to help you deal with them.

Going to court

Most divorces – or to be accurate, the financial aspects of the vast majority of most divorces – are settled without the need to go to court. But if you and your ex look as though you're heading for a contested hearing, there may be steps you can take to halt the proceedings, even at this late stage. You may feel that *not* going to court would be a massive climb-down, or that having your day in court is the only way to get justice. But if you do end up in court, the only people who are certain to gain are the lawyers (because they're paid for their time whatever the outcome).

The only reason you should end up in court is because you've tried everything else or because your ex refuses to settle. You must be prepared for the fact that your legal costs will rise – and very sharply. One divorcee I spoke to paid £1,000 for a meeting with a barrister and another £1,000 for an hour's representation in court. Legal costs running into thousands of pounds are not unusual.

Troubleshooting tips

Try to stay in control

While researching this book, I've spoken to a number of people who have been through or are going through a divorce, and a few of them told me they felt pushed into asking for a bigger settlement or taking a more aggressive stance by their divorce lawyer. Some solicitors who deal with divorce are much more enlightened than they used to be (especially if they belong to Resolution, use mediation or collaborative law), but a few still seem to see it as their job to make the divorce a bigger battleground than it needs to be. Your divorce lawyer is there to give you the benefit of his or her professional expertise, but you should try not to let yourself get swept along into doing something you don't want to.

It's easy to lose a sense of perspective when you're getting divorced. At the time, even the most straightforward letter may feel as if it's designed to be hurtful. Sometimes friends and family will advise you to 'go for every penny you can get' or to stop your ex from 'taking you to the cleaners'. On top of that, our legal system is adversarial: essentially, it's a fight with legal language thrown in. If possible, try to take a step back from what's going on. Ask yourself how you'll feel when all this is over. The wrong reason to continue fighting is that you're angry and you think going to court will make it better. Is that what you *really* want, or would you rather not fight to the end, but be able to rebuild your life a little sooner?

Don't use the courts for revenge

You may want to have your day in court so that you can tell everyone just how badly your ex has behaved, and it's true that some people can be almost unimaginably heartless and cruel during a divorce. But the court is not the right arena to deal with how you feel. The judge isn't interested in the emotional journey you've been on, only in what he or she thinks is a fair settlement. And his or her opinion may be *very* different to your own.

If you do go to court, you may find you run out of money earlier than you anticipated. Some people choose to represent themselves – called being a 'litigant in person' – either because they think they'll do a better job or to save money (Heather Mills is a recent example). If you end up representing yourself, for whatever reason, it's worth knowing that you're allowed to take someone into court to support you through the process, called a 'McKenzie friend'. A McKenzie friend can take notes, whisper questions for you to ask and – most importantly – make sure you don't get too emotional. If you use a McKenzie friend, take someone who's able to calm you down as you're likely to need it. If you can't find anyone, you can hire a McKenzie friend for around £500 a day through www.itsmydivorce.co.uk.

Serious debt problems

For a number of couples, debt and divorce go hand in hand. For many of those who experience debt, it's a short-term problem that they're able to work their way out of, but in a minority of cases the debts can begin to spiral out of control. The problem is that you may not recognise the signs. So how do you know whether your debt problems are temporary or long term? If you're doing any of the things listed below, it's time to seek advice from the debt advice organisations mentioned on p. 143 in Chapter 8.

- You're only making the minimum repayments on your credit cards; you can't afford to pay more and you know that's not likely to change.
- You're using credit cards for everyday items such as groceries (and not to benefit from the interest-free period, but because you have to).
- You're thinking about borrowing more money to 'get yourself out of trouble', although you're not sure how you'll pay it back.

Debt advisers will be able to help you draw up a repayment plan if you cannot afford to pay your loans and debts in full and – more importantly – will prioritise your debts. Some creditors are able to take far more drastic action (such as repossessing your home in the case of mortgage lenders, or sending round bailiffs if you owe council tax) than others. But often the company that sends the most threatening- sounding letters has very little power to follow them up with action.

One of the biggest advantages of using a debt advice charity is that they can deal directly with the companies you owe money to, if you prefer. People who get into debt tell me that one of the most stressful aspects about it is dealing with the telephone calls from banks and other creditors. Sometimes the calls are designed to assist the person who owes money, but I can't help feeling that a lot of the time they aren't. Debt advice charities will be able to take a large part of that anxiety away.

Repossession

Selling the former matrimonial home is bad enough, but facing the prospect of losing it because you can't keep up the repayments can be truly frightening. What I believe many homeowners don't realise is just how small the arrears can be before the lender will start threatening to repossess the property. Lenders will normally mention repossession in their correspondence when you've missed just two payments. If you have short-term cash flow problems, ask your lender if you can take a 'payment holiday' if you have a flexible mortgage (where you don't make any payments for a number of months). Or if you have a repayment loan, you might be able to switch it to an interest-only basis, which will reduce your monthly payments. Some lenders will also extend the term of the loan to give you longer to pay it off. Your first step is to contact them to see what they can do to help.

If you spot the early signs that your mortgage is unaffordable, it might be better to sell up and buy something cheaper (or even rent for a while). However, depending on the housing market, your home could take some time to sell. If you need to sell in a hurry, you could consider a property auction, especially if your house has an unusual layout or needs some work. I've reported on several auctions and had properties valued by surveyors only to see them sell for far more when bidding fever kicks in. However, you have to be careful when setting the reserve price (the price below which it can't be sold) or you could end up getting far less than you'd like.

Vet an auctioneer in the same way you would an estate agent. Ask how many properties the firm has sold at recent auctions and (more importantly) how many remained unsold. What prices did they achieve? You should be able to find out this information by looking on their websites.

If that's not enough to get you out of trouble, talk to a specialist debt adviser who deals with housing debt. The Consumer Credit Counselling Service (www.cccs.co.uk) has set up a mortgage and repossession advice service. In some cases your only option may be to allow the property to be repossessed, but make sure you explore all other avenues with expert help first. If you get to the stage of having a repossession hearing in court, try to attend if you can. If you don't go, the decisions will all be made in in your absence. However, it's much better to go to a repossession hearing after you've taken advice from a reputable debt advice agency.

Sometimes, legal charities will attend the hearing with you, which should mean you're more likely to make a realistic and sustainable offer to repay arrears. Debt advisers say lenders sometimes try to pressurise borrowers into agreeing to repay the arrears more quickly than they can afford to. This is something to be avoided at all costs.

WHEN COURT IS THE ONLY OPTION

'There was a period of five months where my solicitor sent letter after letter and we didn't hear a thing back from my husband. My husband would wait until the day we were due in court before he'd bother to settle. It's all very well being told to be reasonable, but if the other side wants to fight, you've got no option but to fight back. We started divorce proceedings just over eight months ago and already my legal fees are £12,000.'

Cohabiting couples

WHAT'S MINE . . .

'When we broke up, it was impossible to sort out who should get what. There was so much anger and very little positive communication. On top of that, we'd never really discussed or written down how the flat and other things we owned should be divided. After that I decided that I would move in with someone only if we had some sort of written agreement. It's just too difficult without one.'

The main difference between the consequences of getting divorced from a spouse and splitting up with someone you live with is that there's far less certainty about the legal situation when it involves a live-in relationship. There's also no single framework for resolving disputes between couples who live together and so using the law to deal with these issues can be complex. The situation in England, Wales and Northern Ireland is broadly similar, so I will treat those all as one block. Scotland is the only part of the UK that gives cohabiting couples specific rights, so I'll look at the Scottish system separately.

For a while, it seemed as though cohabiting couples in England and Wales would get greater rights, but while I was working on this book, the government announced that it was shelving any changes while it carried out further research into how the Scottish system works. So change may be on the way, but not for the foreseeable future, which means it's even more important that you get to grips with the complexities of the laws that govern who gets what when cohabiting couples break up (or at least that you know where to turn for help). To get an overview of your rights, I'd recommend you visit Advicenow's website (www.advicenow.org.uk). It has a useful section for cohabiting couples who are splitting up, including a 'breaking up checklist' and an extensive question and answer page.

First steps to take

If you have children, maintenance for them will be covered by the CSA (or its replacement, C-MEC) in the same way as if you were married, so turn to Chapter 4 to read up on what to expect. You may also be able to make capital claims on behalf of children (under schedule 1 of the Children Act 1969) to cover costs such as housing. However, these claims are very limited as they only make provision while the children are financially dependent. Any money paid on this basis has to be paid back once the children are no longer dependent.

> Although you can get support for your children, your ex doesn't have to pay you anything even if you gave up work to look after them. Partners can also take away possessions they bought with their own money (unless it was a gift, in which case it belongs to the recipient).

If you own property jointly with your ex partner, you'll also be entitled to a percentage of its value. The amount you will get will depend on how you own it; whether it's as joint tenants or tenants in common (or whether it has a survivorship clause, in Scotland). The value of items you bought together, such as a car or furniture, is likely to be split according to the percentage each of you contributed. However, in the early days your priority will probably be to decide who lives where and to make sure that bills are paid.

You may need to do some or all of these:

- Work out who will move out and who will stay in the home you've been sharing. If you have been living in a rented flat and the tenancy is in your partner's name, you may have very little option but to move.
- Decide who will pay the bills from the home you've shared.
- Contact your mortgage lender to tell them what has happened.
- Contact your bank if you have joint accounts and your credit card company if your partner is a secondary card holder.

Dividing property you own

What happens to property you have shared will depend on who owns it and how it was owned. The options are:

- property owned by one partner
- property owned jointly as joint tenants
- property owned jointly as tenants in common

Property owned by one partner

If the home you've shared is owned by your partner and you've not made any payments towards the mortgage or bills or had an agreement to share, you could find it very difficult — if not impossible — to show you're entitled to any of its value. The only exception would be if you had given up work in order to look after your child/children and expected that you would own a percentage of the home by doing so. If you've not made a financial contribution, you would have to establish that you've got an interest in the property under an implied trust. There are different types of implied trusts:

- resulting trust: where you can claim back financial contributions you have made to the property;
- constructive trust: where you have an agreement to share and have acted on the basis of that agreement.

Normally there would have to be a financial contribution as well. You don't have to have an agreement to share in writing, which is just as well because it's something that many couples probably wouldn't get round to doing. It could be an understanding based on a 'don't worry, this is our house' type of conversation.

However, if you paid part of the mortgage, put money towards building work or renovations or paid the bills while your partner paid the mortgage – and there was an understanding that you would be entitled to a percentage of the property – you should be able to make a claim. The bad news is that this is a very complicated area. If you can afford it, I would suggest that you get in touch with a solicitor who specialises in cohabitation.

If your ex partner owns the house and he or she is declared bankrupt, the creditors may be able to force the sale of the property and evict you. Don't delay if you think this could be an issue; contact a solicitor who specialises in bankruptcy and find out what your options are.

Property owned jointly as joint tenants

Owning your property as joint tenants means you own it equally between you. You are each entitled to 50 per cent of its value when you break up, no matter who paid the mortgage, and one partner will inherit the remaining 50 per cent if the other dies, no matter what is written in the will. If you don't know how your home is owned, your first port of call should be the Land Registry (www.landregisteronline.gov.uk) to see what the title deeds say. For a £3 fee, you can check the title deeds online. If they just list your names and address, it is likely that you own the property as joint tenants. If they have your names and address, followed by a 'restriction', you probably own it as tenants in common. Family lawyers tell me that occasionally details are registered incorrectly on the Land Register, so it may be worth double-checking how the property is owned via a second source. You could ask for a copy of the transfer form (TR1), which was introduced in 1998 and which spells out who has an interest in a property.

It is possible for you to change the way you own property from joint tenants to tenants in common by serving a notice of severance. The details are outlined on p. 90 in Chapter 5.

Property owned as tenants in common

Owning your home as tenants in common gives you the chance to specify how much each of you possesses. However, you shouldn't assume that just because you buy as tenants in common that you automatically have unequal shares. A court case that went as far as the House of Lords in 2007 spelt out the importance of having an agreement (called a 'declaration of trust') drawn up when you buy. Unless you specify who owns what, the assumption will still be that you split ownership of the property 50 : 50.

If you have a declaration of trust, it should include both who owns what percentage of the property and what should happen if you and your partner were to split up. If those safeguards are in place, it should be *relatively* straightforward working out what happens.

It doesn't matter whether one of you is planning to buy the other out, or you are hoping to sell up. Your first step should be to get your property valued by three different estate agents. Selling up to buy two different properties gives both of you an incentive to maximise the sale price, but if one of you is buying the other out, there could be different agendas at work here. There's more information about how you can come off a joint mortgage and how to unravel your property-related finances in Chapter 5.

Rented property

If you share a rented house or flat with your partner, the rights you have depend on the type of rental agreement and whose name the tenancy is in. The most common type of tenancies in the private rented and housing association sector are assured and assured shorthold tenancies. With an assured tenancy, you have far greater rights than with an assured shorthold agreement (where the landlord can regain possession six months after the start of the tenancy, provided you are given two months' notice).

Tenancy in joint names: private sector

If the rental agreement is in both your names, you should be able to take it over if your partner leaves and vice versa. However, it does mean that you're both responsible for the rent until the agreement is changed to a sole name, so you would need to be sure that the partner remaining in the property has the means to pay the rent and intends to do so.

> There was a major shake-up of the rental sector in 1989, which saw the creation of assured shorthold tenancies. For the purposes of simplicity, I'm going to treat all tenancies as though they started after 1989. If yours didn't, I suggest you take specialist advice, either by contacting Shelter through their website at www.shelter.org.uk (or by telephoning them on 0808 800 4444 if you need urgent help) or by getting in touch with your local Citizens Advice. Their contact details are listed in Yellow Pages, or you can find details at www.adviceguide.org.uk.)

Most private rental agreements start out as 'fixed term' tenancies, often for six months or a year, but once they have been renewed, they change to 'periodic' tenancies (which have no specific end date). If you have a fixed term tenancy and you want to leave before the agreement is up, you and your partner have to agree to end the tenancy with your landlord. With a periodic tenancy, either of you can give notice to the landlord.

Once you have given notice, it brings your tenancy to an end and it could mean you have to move out and find somewhere else to live. To get round this, contact the landlord and ask if he or she will give you a new tenancy in your name only. Make sure you have something in writing from your landlord before you give notice on the joint tenancy.

Tenancy in joint names: council housing

If you have a council tenancy in joint names, you should contact the council to see what the options are. They may agree to change it to one of your names only, but they're not obliged to.

With both private and council tenancies, the courts can order the transfer of a tenancy from one cohabiting partner to another when a relationship breaks down. It normally only happens when someone has been a victim of domestic violence, or when there's a risk that they would be homeless without the court order (if they care for the children). However, the courts cannot order the transfer of a tenancy once the landlord has been given notice.

Tenancy in sole name

If the tenancy is in your name only, you can ask your partner to leave. The rules state that you should give him or her what is called 'reasonable notice' (for example, a minimum of 28 days if rent is paid monthly). If, on the other hand, the rental agreement is in your name but you don't want to remain in the flat, your partner could ask the landlord for a new rental agreement in their name.

If you're taking over your partner's tenancy agreement, you will have to be able to demonstrate that you can afford the rent. If the rent was previously paid out of a joint account (rather than your partner's), so much the better; if not, you'll have to come up with evidence, such as a bank reference, to show you can afford it.

Scotland

A change in the law in 2006 means that couples who live together in Scotland have specific rights and obligations.

- If you believe you have been economically disadvantaged (by, for example, giving up work during the relationship to look after your children), you may be able to make a claim through the courts against your ex partner.
- If you benefited from your partner economically during the relationship, you may have a claim made against you.
- If you have children together and you have the economic burden of caring for them, you can make a claim through the courts against your ex-partner.
- If you and your partner cannot divide household goods bought while you were together, the law will assume you own them jointly.

The courts will consider how long you lived together, what type of relationship you had and the financial arrangements you made during your relationship (for example, did you have joint bank accounts and support each other financially?). Not all property is treated the same way. Your house would not be presumed to belong to you jointly, for example, and you should check how the title to the property is held.

Many couples are still unaware of their rights and what it could mean for them. In particular, you may be able to raise an action under Scots law even if you don't live in Scotland. If you or your partner has any connection to Scotland (if either of you were born or live there, say), you should get good advice from a solicitor about what rights you may have. Another area that could catch out couples who split up is the time limit: you can only bring a claim against your ex-partner within the first year after you break up and within six months after they die.

WHO DECIDES WHAT'S FAIR

'I owned my own house and when Simon moved in, he said he didn't want to pay rent because that would mean that if we split up he would have some rights on my property. I'm not sure whether he was right or whether he was just trying to avoid chipping in. I never asked for rent money after that and he hardly paid me anything towards the food bills. He was so defensive about it all, but when we split up I did realise I'd been paying almost all of the bills for both of us.'

12 Moving on

After your divorce

The chances are that you will have filled in so many forms and had to make so many financial decisions during your divorce that you probably won't want to make any more. But, while your divorce may be over, there are some steps you should take to make sure your finances get – and stay – on track. If you were able to manage your money at a difficult and stressful time, you should find it a lot easier once that's over. This chapter will help you understand what your financial priorities should be and will point you in the right direction if you would like to know more.

Steps to financial happiness

- Pay off debts
- Monitor your spending
- Start saving
- Protect yourself
- Invest for your future

Pay off debts

Chapter 8 has already covered debt problems, but if your financial situation has improved, perhaps because you've received some money from the sale of your house or through maintenance payments, now is the time to develop some sound money management strategies. The first step is to pay off your debts.

If you're being charged interest, the most efficient way to do this is to pay off the one that charges the highest rate of interest first. Switch credit cards to 0 per cent balance transfer deals if you can. Next, pay the maximum you can afford on the loan or credit card charging the highest rate of interest and the minimum you can on the rest without breaking the terms of the contract. Work your way through your agreements one by one. If you get any extra money or receive a pay rise, increase your repayments.

If you pay off all your debts and never borrow again, you may find your credit rating isn't good enough to let you get credit when you actually need it. So if you have a credit card, my advice is to use it, but only if you don't buy anything you wouldn't normally or that you can't afford, and to pay off your balance in full every month. If you don't have a card, it may be worth applying for one to boost your rating further (and two cards will give you a higher score than one). But stick to the guidelines I've mentioned.

Monitor your spending

If you're finding it hard to pay back your loans and you're not sure where your money is going, try keeping a spending diary. The idea is that you write down how much you spend, what you spend it on and when you spend it over a period of a few months. It may be that you simply don't have enough money to go round and there's little room for cutbacks. But sometimes it can help to write down exactly what you're spending and how much those impulse buys really cost. For many of us, money isn't just a practical way of paying for things we need, it's something we have an emotional response to.

You may spend money when you're stressed or feeling down as a means of consolation or, when things are going well, as a treat or reward. Getting divorced is one of the most stressful experiences you're ever likely to go through. So if you know you're the kind of person who has a tendency to spend when you're stressed, maybe you should leave your credit card at home when you go shopping or ask a friend to keep an eye on your spending for you.

I'm not trying to say that you should cut down on all but the absolute necessities, but if you buy treats you can't afford, you'll only add to the stress of divorce. Most of us, even if we happily skip to the shops with a handful of credit cards, don't enjoy being faced with bills we can't afford to pay.

Start saving

Once you've paid off your debts, start saving. If you already have some money set aside, work out whether it's enough to keep you going if there's a financial problem around the corner. You should aim for enough savings to cover your outgoings for three months, but if that seems like a tall order, save what you can. Some money is better than none at all. Use the FSA's comparative tables and/or price comparison sites I mentioned in Chapter 8 to find a savings account that pays a good rate.

The Financial Services Compensation Scheme is there to protect savers so that they don't lose out if a bank or building society fails. At the time of writing, the government planned to make changes to it so that the first £50,000 of savings (rather than the old limit of £35,000) per person is protected. That limit could either be £50,000 per person per bank, or £50,000 per 'brand' as some banks provide accounts for several brands (for example, HBOS owns Birmingham Midshires, Halifax and IF).

Protect yourself

Divorce in England, Wales and Northern Ireland does not invalidate a will, but your ex will not receive assets you have left them in your will. However, divorce does nothing to stop your possessions from passing to your ex's relatives, if that's what you have specified in your will. In Scotland, divorce does not revoke a will. Wherever you live, the best advice is to draw up a new one – and sooner rather than later.

Doing it yourself with an off-the-shelf pack is the cheapest option, but there's a danger that you may make a mistake. If you want to use a solicitor, make sure you choose one who specialises in will and probate. You can search for one on the Law Society website (www.lawsociety.org.uk for England and Wales and www.lawscot.org.uk for Scotland), if you don't have a personal recommendation.

Will writers are an alternative to solicitors, but they don't have to have any training or take out professional insurance unless they're members of the Institute of Professional Willwriters (www.ipw.org.uk). Getting a will drawn up by a will writer or a solicitor doesn't have to be expensive. You could expect to pay £75–£150 for a straightforward will, although drawing up a complicated and tax-efficient one could cost several hundred pounds.

If you're sorting out your will, you should also think about setting up a Lasting Power of Attorney (LPA), which sets out who will make decisions about your finances and your health should you become incapable of doing so. It's not the cheeriest of subjects, but it's well worth thinking about. The bad news is that LPAs are not cheap, so check with your professional will writer or solicitor exactly how much it will cost.

> Don't forget life insurance, either for yourself or to cover maintenance payments you may be receiving or any debts such as a mortgage. Most life insurance policies pay out a lump sum when the policyholder dies, but it may be more appropriate (and cheaper) for you to take out a 'family income benefit' policy, which pays a tax-free monthly income from the claim until the end of the term.

Invest in your future

You may have received a lump sum as part of your divorce settlement and wonder what to do with it. The simple answer is that you don't have to do anything in a hurry. Investment decisions are something you should take for the longer term, so there's no harm in leaving any money you have in a savings account for a few months while you work out what you want to do with it and what advice you'd like (if any).

If you want to get advice on how to invest your money, I'd suggest you see an independent financial adviser (IFA) who has to look at products available from the whole market and give you the option of paying for the advice by fee or a commission. There are two other types of adviser ('tied' and 'multi-tied'), but both are likely to be paid a small salary and rely heavily on commission. They also won't be able to pick the best products from the market as they are tied to one company (in the case of a tied adviser) or can sell the products of around half-a-dozen different providers (if the adviser is multi-tied).

You can find details of IFAs near your home or place of work by looking on the website of IFA promotions (www.unbiased.co.uk). You select an IFA by different criteria, but the site can't tell you if they're any good. Ask friends and family for a personal recommendation; otherwise be prepared to vet your IFA. Trust your instincts. If you think they're more concerned about their own pocket than your financial future (or even if they can't explain financial terms very well), go somewhere else. You may have to make some important financial decisions, so don't use someone you're not completely comfortable with.

Looking forward to your future

When I've been talking to people who've been through divorce and come out the other side, they have one thing in common: they're able to look forward, not back. They may not be living the life they expected, but they're able to plan for the future – their own future. There are moments of sadness and anger, but they're countered by happiness and hope. I'm not saying it's easy, but don't imagine that life won't get better. Believe me, it will.

AFTER THE DIVORCE

'What I tried to do was, in effect, to act as if the divorce was five years behind us and we'd sorted things out. I wanted to think about how my life would be then and what I could do to make sure it was a life I wanted to lead. It's meant lots of frustration and compromise and I went against a lot of people's advice to 'get the hell out' and 'go for what I could'. But now I can begin to focus on my future — and that's a good feeling!'

Index